A Book For Couples

OTHER BOOKS BY HUGH PRATHER

Notes to Myself
I Touch the Earth, the Earth Touches Me
Notes on Love and Courage
There Is a Place Where You Are Not Alone
A Book of Games: A Course in Spiritual Play
The Quiet Answer
Notes on How to Live in the World . . .
   and Still Be Happy

A
Book
For
Couples

HUGH and GAYLE PRATHER

Doubleday
New York
1988

Library of Congress Cataloging-in-Publication Data
Prather, Hugh.
    A book for couples.
    1. Marriage.   2. Interpersonal relations.
3. Love.   I. Prather, Gayle.   II. Title.
HQ734.P84   1987   306.8′1   83-45343
ISBN 0-385-18785-8

A SPECIAL ACKNOWLEDGMENT . . .

to Colt Lintecum for being a friend to our boys during the two years this book was in the making. His gentle care of our children allowed us to write happily, and surely a trace of his lovely spirit runs throughout these pages.

CONTENTS

SECTION I

THE WHOLE OF YOUR RELATIONSHIP

Introduction   3

CHAPTER I

YOU COULDN'T HAVE PICKED
A MORE DIFFICULT TIME   5

Are You Sure It Was a Mistake?   5
The Function of Hope   8
A Widespread and Mistaken Approach   9
Once We Had Rules   12
The Ego's Need to Separate   13
The Power of Unity   15
Emotions True and False   17

CHAPTER II

WHO WOULD IT TAKE
TO MAKE LOVE POSSIBLE?   20

Letting Go of Romance   20
The Fiction of the Well-Matched Pair   21
The Road to Your One Great Love   23
The Gentle Use of the Mind   25

CHAPTER III

LETTING GO OF DIFFERENCES   28

The Old You Cannot Begin Anew   28
Trying to Match the Superficials   29
Your List of Unjoinables   32

Specialness Must Be Defended   33
Being Un-different Together   36
Watching Without Judgment   37
Triggering Sadness—Triggering Peace   39

CHAPTER IV

WHICH RELATIONSHIP ARE YOU IN?   43

The Center Path   43
Love Is Always Like Itself   45
The Inherited Way of Looking   46
Seeing Naturally   48
Comparisons Hold No Kindness   49
Seeing One Who Is Not There   50
No One Is Unable to Commit   52
A Relationship Cannot Give   53
Below the Sentence Level of the Mind   54
Begin at the Ending Point   56

SECTION II

THE PARTS OF YOUR RELATIONSHIP

Introduction   63

CHAPTER V

FREEING THE RELATIONSHIP
FROM ITS PAST   66

The Effort to Appear Normal   66
What Is Unforgivable?   68
How Many Alterations Does Your Partner Need?   71
Your Preoccupations Transform You   73
How Hard Does Your Partner Work to Torment You?   75
How Poison Enters the Mind   77
Seeing the Blocks to Happiness   80

Recording the Blocks to Happiness   81
Alerting Yourself to the Blocks to Happiness   83
Examining the Blocks to Happiness   84
Discarding the Blocks to Happiness   86
The Source of Freedom   89

CHAPTER VI

HOW TO RESOLVE ISSUES UNMEMORABLY   91

Unfinished Arguments Accumulate   91
Each New Issue Resurrects the Old   93
Discussions Create the Relationship's Terrain   94
The Magic Rules for Ruining Any Discussion   96
To Agree Is Not the Purpose   98
Five Steps in Preparing to Argue   101
The Six Rules of Arguing   106
Resolving Issues Within Yourself   114
Study, Humility, and Concentration   116

CHAPTER VII

SETTLED PATTERNS AND
UNHAPPY DYNAMICS   118

Blind Commitment   118
Unlearning the Roles of Husband and Wife   121
Presuming Mutual Participation   123
The Answer to Every Call for Help Is
Gentleness   125
Insight: A Gift or a Weapon?   127
Neither Bait nor Rise to the Bait   129
The Symptom of Feeling Separate   130
"You Are Never Upset for the Reason You
Think"   132
Identifying the Problem's Veneer   134
The Promise Sustains the Pain   135
Stay Focused on a Single Thread   136

A Brief Case History   138
One Underlying Dynamic   143
Symbols of Your Sincerity   145

CHAPTER VIII

COMMON PROBLEMS   148

One Problem—One Answer   148

SEX
How's Your Sex Life   152
Four Qualities Essential to Success   154
Observation and Options   158
Detailing the First Plan   159
Summary   162

JEALOUSY AND TRUST
Jealousy's Counterpart   163
Being Attractive   164
Pathological Jealousy   166
Trust Is Not Control   166
Specific Steps   167
Your Partner's Place in Your Mind   168

AFFAIRS
A Symbol and Its Effect   169
What Are You Going to Do About It?   170
Making a Decision   172
Revenge Fantasies   173
The Affair and Its Effects Are One   174
Suffering Is a Request for Love   175
Your Joint Plan for Healing   176

FINANCES
Treasuring Your Relationship   178
Undercutting Money   179
Row Gently   181

HAVING CHILDREN
Children Are Wonderful and Much More   182
A Baby Will Not Perk Up Your Relationship   184
Common Dynamics   185
Another Spouse's Children   188

"I NEED MY OWN SPACE"
Mental Separateness   190
Using a Symbol's Power   191
Ways of Joining   194
Helping Make It Easier   196

GROWING OLD TOGETHER
Your Partner Is a Mirror   198
Become As a Child   200
The Body's Function   201
Opportunity of a Lifetime   202

EPILOGUE

THE LAST INSTRUCTION   207

SECTION I

The Whole of
Your Relationship

INTRODUCTION

We do not see the relationship. We see merely the other individual and his or her faults. We stand on top of half the relationship to look at the other half, and our perspective determines our opinion of the whole. We look at differences, not at oneness. We look at separation, not at love.

Most of those who have been married can probably remember being asked, "How's married life?" by some friend they encountered a short time after the service. The honeymoon stage was not yet over and their answer was bright and hopeful. (One knows not to enquire after the first year or two.) If you ask yourself that question now notice the tendency to appraise only your spouse and only in terms of whether he or she is giving you what you want and need. The attitude is very much like two men rating the performance of a car.

"How's she holding up?"

"She's got fifty thousand miles on her and still only needs one quart between changes!"

"That's great. Better not trade her in."

"No, I think I'll keep her awhile."

We spoke to a friend recently who had discarded his wife of over thirty years and married again. He said, "The new one gives me what the old one didn't. She really looks after me. All she wants is to make me happy." We were startled that he didn't even use the individuals' names—until we realized that he was merely stating a common attitude in blunt language.

So what is the alternative? The vital question is not "How is married life (treating you)?" but "How are you and your partner treating your relationship?" The relationship was created by two people. Before they came together, it did not exist. It is shaped and sustained by their love, or lack of it. It is like a candle they hold between them, lighting their way through the world. They must walk gently and side by side or the winds of the times will most assuredly extinguish it, and in their hands will be a thing that merely smokes and smells and then grows cold.

A theme that Gayle and I will return to many times in this book is that the two of you are not the relationship. Otherwise there would be no difference if you were single and had never met. Something new now exists and it will continue even if your bodies separate permanently. It is part of your mind, of course, and it will drain or strengthen you depending on whether you nurture it from your heart or your ego. If you can see this clearly you will instinctively rush to help each other rather than turn away, and once that reaction becomes habitual, you will be at one with a great love and a lasting friendship.

CHAPTER I

You Couldn't Have Picked a More Difficult Time

Are You Sure It Was a Mistake?

Gayle and I did not get off to a particularly good start.

In 1965 I had returned to college to get a teaching certificate and was living in an apartment in Dallas with two single friends. We were without companions and too shy to do much about it. However, living next door were three women who evidently spent every night screaming, singing, listening to country music, and perhaps even doing everything else we fantasized as we pressed water glasses against the adjoining wall in an attempt to fill in the lurid details.

Strange men came and went at all hours, and apparently there was a small dog who was never let out and whose frenzied yelps punctuated all the other muffled and irregular sounds.

You would think that three so obviously accessible women living only inches away would have solved all our problems. But, as I said, we were very shy. Although we analyzed their behavior exhaustively, we made no overtures. Then there was a misunderstanding.

One night, at 2 A.M., the long-legged one named Gayle knocked on our front door. She handed David a box of blank checks that she said she had picked up by mistake from the mail bin. The next morning the three of us discussed the true meaning of this remarkable event. Since they were my checks, and since there was no reason for her to have returned them at such a provocative hour (aside from night being as day to the women next door), David and Jim argued that this was a come-on directed at me, that I had been chosen and a counter-move on my part was in order. I admitted that their logic was impeccable.

But don't forget, I was shy; so shy, in fact, that I talked David, who was very eloquent, into going over and asking Gayle to have a date with me. To my surprise, he succeeded.

So Gayle and I had our date, but it turned out that her boyfriend had stolen the box, and when he told her that he was going to write hot checks, she had waited until he went to the bathroom and snuck them next door. The reason she had agreed to our date, she explained, was that she thought I had a glass eye. I quickly saw (with both eyes) that Gayle was everything I had imagined and asked her for a second date.

But when I asked her for a third, my roommates became concerned and each inquired if I was getting serious.

Their questions appalled me. The three of us, I pointed out, were on a spiritual path, whereas Gayle listened to country-western music. We had tossed salads and blender drinks. Gayle drank large bottles of Dr Pepper and had white-flour pizza delivered to her door. The litany went on and on until I was certain they understood my consistency in all matters, and also the real reason for my dating her: She had long legs and, although not yet revealing this side to me, was patently a very wild young woman.

My mental clarity intact, I took Gayle out that night to a coffee house that was featuring a popular local singer whom neither of us had heard. We pulled up across the street, and I turned off the ignition. We sat there staring blankly ahead. I noticed that we were not getting out. Finally I turned to her and said, "Do you really want to go in?"

"No, I don't think so."

"Well," I said, "would you like to get married?"

She considered this for a second or two and said, "Well, I guess so."

I had long wondered what a psychotic break felt like and now I knew the universe was answering my question.

In 1965 one could not get married quickly in Texas, yet it is very important to take advantage of a psychotic break while it lasts. Therefore, after stopping at Gayle's apartment for a mostly white dress, we headed straight for the Oklahoma border where they stayed up all night just waiting for the moonstruck to arrive.

On the way there we didn't talk much, but out of a sudden curiosity I did ask Gayle if she thought the marriage would work. "No," she said, "it probably won't. What do you think?"

My feeling was a little more definite, having thought the whole matter through for the benefit of my roommates just that afternoon. So, having agreed and put that question to rest, we proceeded on to the border.

At three in the morning Mr. and Mrs. Raymond Grimes, one of an ocean of justices of the peace, married us in their pajamas, wished us well, and went back to sleep.

During the long drive back my only consoling thought was that at last I was going to experience first-hand Gayle's passionate side, which she had been hiding from me so cleverly. As if reading my mind, she turned and said, "Of course you realize, no piece of paper gives any man the right to my body."

And with that pronouncement she made me drive her back to her own apartment, which she entered without so much as a kiss good night, and refused to see me for two weeks. (Although we did talk twice on the phone.)

The Function of Hope

We both thought we had made a mistake, and in many ways we seemed to set out to prove it. The first fourteen or so years of our marriage were by no means all bad, but they were typical of many marriages in that we never became each other's absolute friend. That we did not lose hope was atypical. We stayed together and we kept trying.

Please do not misunderstand. We do not advocate staying together at all costs. Time alone will not bring about a real relationship. Clearly there have been divorces that were needed. But if you have not yet broken up, possibly your situation is not as extreme as you may believe and your sanity might be better served if you would devote yourself for a time to trying in every possible way. This you cannot do while entertaining questions of whether you should leave, whether there is someone better, whether you missed your time to indulge in the single life, and so forth.

While it remains apparent to you that you are not doing all you could, your mind is in a poor position to justify leaving. At best it can only ask a question for which you have not yet provided a complete answer. There is a natural sense of "now is the time to leave," but it never comes as a question. It arises from the heart, not from fear and discontent. This self-loving and caring instinct is *not* masked by your loving and caring for another. Therefore trust your heart that if ever it is best to leave, you will know that when the time comes, and unless that occurs, you will assume that the potential is still there and you will work as if its fulfillment is entrusted to you personally.

Although Gayle and I use the example of marriage most often, we have written this book for any two who wish to begin forming a deep and enduring relationship, regardless of the time already spent otherwise. We want you to know that we are acutely conscious of how difficult this process can be. If we had not used so similar a title in our last book, we would have called this one "How to Live with Someone and Still Be Happy," because it can seem an almost impossible task.

Short of a separation, the answer to the unhappy state that most relationships fall into is typically sought in various forms of withdrawal and distance. If this solution is motivated by an underlying arrogance, as it almost always is, it can make one's home a place to escape rather than the haven from the world it should be. Gayle and I are aware of this not only from years of counseling other couples but from first-hand experience with a sometimes strained and troubled marriage. We have written this book because we have proved to ourselves that deep enjoyment of another can be the consistent fact of one's life. A time can come when you know that your partner will never desert you, that you *have* a partner, someone to walk beside you, someone with whom you can grow old.

This potential is in stark contrast to the values of our time. I tell you plainly that it could only have been proved to me by direct experience. I thought I knew absolutely that continuously growing happiness between two people was not remotely possible and that those who claimed it were in some kind of false honeymoon period, were stupidly self-deceived, or were dangerously dishonest. Hope is tremendously important, and if this book does nothing more than give you hope—enough of it that you are willing to try—it will have served its purpose well. Our promise to you is that if you will work in a direct and simple way, you can come to know love, you can come to have peace, and your home at last will be a place of true rest. But do not underestimate the world's deep disbelief in this opportunity and its effect on your motivation.

A Widespread and Mistaken Approach

At present, most "serious" romantic relationships are lasting only a few months and most marriages only a few years. This is not a tragedy but it does indicate an erroneous approach, since all these couples had intended to stay together. Gayle and I became increasingly familiar with the mistakes that were being made as our counseling "practice" (in quotes because we do not charge) shifted from crisis and grief to marriage and its modern equivalents. This shift occurred, as do so many of life's more helpful changes, in a rather roundabout and unpremeditated way.

In the late seventies we were working on a twenty-four-hour crisis intervention hot line and running a support group for parents in grief as well as facilitating a general support group for battered women, rape victims, the suicidal and others in crisis, but as the months went by, Gayle and I saw that although we were patching up many people, within a few weeks or months they would find themselves in still another crisis. In short, no real change was occurring in their lives, and it was obvious that our help had to go much deeper.

We decided that the most effective thing we personally could do would be to teach an overall approach to life in a thorough and systematic way.[1] Sunday seemed to be a day when most were free to attend, and so several of us from the support groups rented space from the Santa Fe Girls' Club and I began giving an hour talk there each week. We named our all-volunteer operation The Dispensable Church.[2]

Several months later a woman approached me and said that she and her friend had been coming to the Girls' Club, had fallen in love, and they wanted me to marry them.

"This is wonderful," I said, "but I'm not a minister. Perhaps we could get a minister to co-officiate."

"But you don't understand," she said. "We met while at-

[1] *Notes on How to Live in the World . . . and Still Be Happy* (Doubleday & Co., 1986) is a summary of this teaching written in nonreligious terms.
[2] My three years of talks were taped and the cassettes are available from The Dispensable Church, Box 8444, Santa Fe, New Mexico 87504-8444. Our textbook was *A Course in Miracles* and therefore these talks are religious in tone. (Incidentally, The Dispensable Church is a nonprofit organization. Gayle and I receive no money from it or from the sale of these tapes.)

tending your talks and we fell in love while attending your talks. You are the only person who can marry us."

"Yes, but. . . ."

"And furthermore," she said, "our relationship is sort of platonic until you marry us."

"You're not having sex?" I couldn't decide if this was refreshing or horrifying. In Santa Fe it was certainly unusual.

She smiled shyly but resolutely.

"Well then, I will see what I can do."

I called an attorney friend of mine and explained that there was a couple who insisted that I was the only one who could marry them. "And furthermore," I said, "their relationship is sort of platonic until they get married."

"Does that mean they're not having sex?"

"I think it does."

"I'll have you a minister by the end of the week."

Actually it took three weeks, but by then Gayle and I were both ministers, and the weddings began coming.

The first two we did ended in divorce (one in two weeks, one in about six or eight months), and so we began insisting on seeing any couple who wished us to marry them for at least three counseling sessions before the service took place, and we urged them to be open to calling on us for help afterward. Our record improved as a result, but it leveled off at only a little better than fifty-fifty. On the whole, the people we married had no religious or philosophical reason for keeping a marriage intact. Most of those who attended The Dispensable Church would not have if they had thought of it as a "real" church, so in a sense they were good examples of the unattached, so-called free thinking younger (under fifty) generation of today.[3] It is this group which has probably been most influenced by the ideals of our time, but in our counseling experience we have noticed that those over fifty have been manipulated by

[3] An increasing number are beginning families in their late thirties and even early forties and, as a result, tend to identify themselves with what would have before been thought of as the values of twenty- and thirty-year-olds.

these more than they realize, and of course they have other problems brought from the era in which they grew up.

Once We Had Rules

We have come from a time when most believed in a universal order of behavior. If they lived by the rules they would be happy. Marriage was merely one of the moves in a very complicated but precise dance of life. The general faith was that such a dance existed, that although intricate it was possible to master, and having done so, one could expect to know contentment within one's home, one's job, one's church, one's recreation and so forth. Many of the old reruns on television display this attitude in a very charming way, and it is tempting to think that if we could all return to the mind set of an earlier time we would escape from our present confusion and unhappiness.

But this is not an accurate memory of the way it was. Earlier generations did not have better relationships even though they married more readily and divorced infrequently. This was merely part of the dance. One worked hard, one got married, one had children, and one stayed with one's spouse, one's church and one's political party. Marriages lasted longer not because they held more genuine love but because of the greater fear of divorce, that is, of the consequences of deviating from the prescribed steps. That particular fear has lessened and we find ourselves in a very confusing time, not knowing whether to get married or live together, to work hard at our career or to have children, to change jobs or protect our security. Now that society tells us we are free to do almost anything we wish, now that we have what a dance does not allow us to have—the option to sit it out—we find that we are adrift, pushed by every wave of articles or spate of TV specials into new fears and greater uncertainty.

And yet within this wash of fear comes the urge for closeness, for a sense of reliable and lasting companionship, for a sense of being truly connected. We know we are not happy and yet we still feel in our hearts the one fact that has never changed throughout the ages: that happiness and love cannot be separated. Of course, with our confused sense of self we pervert this into meaning that we cannot be happy until we have the ideal romantic partner. So let us look a little more closely at this longing so many now feel and also at the environment in which it is surfacing.

The Ego's Need to Separate

This is a time when the old ideals have been questioned and when the world itself is being viewed with more honesty. In our long history a great deal has been tried and has not succeeded as expected, and there is now a growing sense of weariness with the world. The mistaken reaction to these newly seen realities is the tremendous emphasis, so unmistakable in all forms of media, on separateness. It is as if by defining and polishing and protecting our personal differences, we can strike to the core of ourselves and find at last a real stability.

Today, within any marriage-type relationship, it is expected that each will have separate but equal careers, separate finances, separate opinions on every important subject, take separate political stands and possibly even separate vacations. This is supposedly a manifestation of greater personal strength. Although it is certainly not strength, in a sense it is more truthful because the one-mindedness that seemed to exist between husband and wife before was mostly manufactured. She deferred to him in all matters except housekeeping and child care, and even though this gave an appearance of order, there was no more unity and love than in most modern relationships.

Stress on individual distinctions asserts the ego and not the heart. The egos of any two people are separate because each comes from a different matrix of childhood experiences. It *is* a form of honesty to see these differences, but if little more than this is done, as is currently the case in virtually all relationships, then loneliness and anger quickly replace the initial feelings of being special and being right that an energetic defense of one's ego-self can bring.

As we use the terms in this book, the *ego* is the superficial and shifting layer of the mind and the *heart* is the deeper core, the true and consistent self. The ego can be thought of as a self-image or an imagined sense of self that arises from an individual's personal history. Its basic characteristics are set in place during the formative years and are reinforced by how later events are perceived. In other words, the child picks up a way of seeing things, substantially from its parents, and all that happens to it seems to confirm these early lessons. The lessons themselves, however, conflict, and so this received identity is unstable. The past does not have a single voice, and thus the ego is a collection of contradictory thoughts. Whenever the mind turns to the ego for direction it experiences anxiety, just as it experiences peace when it turns to the heart.

Sometimes a child's first friend is an imaginary playmate, and it quite naturally may resist any thought of no longer producing this image even though it is a block to real companionship. Being its first sense of self, the child, and later the adult, is even more attached to its ego. It wants this imaginary identity and it wants to serve its interests. It believes that not to do so would destroy its only self, just as to deny its imaginary playmate would leave it friendless. In this book the definition of *selfishness* will be "devotion to one's ego." It is a loveless pursuit because the ego, being a collection of singular experiences, contains nothing that can join with another.

Although we refer to the ego at times as a layer or level or part of the mind, strictly speaking it is a product of the mind and cannot be kept or integrated into the self. It is merely a fantasy, although a very complex one. The mind can and must be freed from this unhappy activity, but the activity itself is neither good nor bad, because the individual's self is not an ego. In the way we will use the term no dualism is implied, no war is called for in weakening and ultimately relinquishing the ego. One increasingly decides to listen to one's heart or real self and has less and less use for selfishness. The ego doesn't go anywhere because it was only imagined, and one is left whole and in position to love.

The Power of Unity

At the same time that we are feeling a strong need to be separate we also sense that somehow relationships are very important to our happiness, and so we are presently trying to have both, to be different but have no differences, to be special but one. All anyone has to do is look around to see how complete a failure this approach is.

The answer lies not in avoiding the usual forms that specialness takes but in gently questioning the *need* to stand apart. This never includes formulating rules of conduct such as not buying clothes of good quality, damping down one's humor, or not seeking advancement in one's occupation. Specialness is the wish to be distinguishable in the eyes of other egos, and although this exhibits itself in behavior, there is no catalogue of actions one must avoid. What must be avoided is thinking of oneself as alone and out of context.

Which need will be served—to be special or to be joined with another? For they are as incompatible as darkness and light. The irony of this supposed clashing of interests is that it is between benefit and the illusion of benefit, for we are not swallowed up but found within a loving relationship. The gift held out to each partner is immense: the opportunity to release a healing brightness that has long been sealed in the heart.

In a real relationship we lift our gaze from our little self to the part of us that is capable of becoming a true friend to another. When the desire to help, to make another feel happy and safe, begins to surface, it is as if we are transmuted— gradually, slowly and with much reinforced effort—from one person into another remarkably incomparable to the first. Fear finally gives way to strength, smallness to love. We find a new set of pleasures far more durable than the old: the pleasure of removing another's anxieties, of bringing comfort and peace, of making home and offering rest.

And who is it that does this? Who are you, what are you, when you love very simply, when you love without ego? You are certainly not the shabby vulnerable lost little creature you may have been reacting against for a very long time. To love another is no reaction. It is a new direction that cannot help spreading its gentle warmth over every aspect of your life. And that is why a true partnership is not an isolated area, even though *most individuals view relationships as something apart from their real life*. To the contrary, a relationship that is steady and true gathers all things and all people into its gentle influence.

The climate being one equally of wanting to be separate and of wanting to feel connected, relationships of necessity are being put under impossible demands. We are due a partner who is devoted and understanding of our needs, one who will join us in our destiny and work alongside us toward our most deeply held goals. And yet the other may look to us for exactly the same things. Or perhaps somewhat different things. Perhaps he or she wants one who can give and share physical pleasure, one who has common interests, a companion and a playmate, one who is young at heart or perhaps even looks young.

So what *can* you expect from a relationship? Nothing at all separately, but together everything that is worth having. The desire for oneness in the home, for happiness, for love can be fulfilled by any two who come together in a state of openness and with a serious willingness to let go of the conflicted and loveless values of our times. A steady resolve to work together, to join hearts, to have no separate pains, no unshared weaknesses, can sweep away the years of troubled times and make the days fresh and new again. There is great power in unity, and the dictum of this world that all of us are ultimately alone will vanish before it like the fog of night before a morning sun.

Couples who think they have managed to join in the pursuit of separateness use their partner as a hand mirror. They look to him or her as a gauge of how their own life is going. If the other shows signs of aging, they feel older, if he or she develops new interests, their old interests and long-standing tastes are brought into question. Like the messenger of old who brought bad news, the partner who is a mirror must be hated and destroyed.

If the goal in life is to be special, how much patience can we have for differences of opinion, for little arguments that go on into the night, for sick children and broken appliances? How understanding can we be of absentmindedness if it involves *our* birthday or of carelessness if it involves *our* car? The modern desire to stand out and stand alone demands a bankrupting price of this other body, this other person, who cannot and will not seek to be special in the same ways we will and so must forever fail to give us our due. There are no joint destinies toward specialness. No one can consistently love another while pursuing such a goal, even though alliances can be formed that appear for a time to serve both parties' separate interests.

Emotions True and False

Most couples just starting out who come to us for counseling have no idea what they are in for if they truly wish to establish a long-term relationship. Today's environment is of course just one of the problems facing any old or new relationship, and we will discuss some others in the next chapter, but the atmosphere of ideas that we breathe in with every headline and coffee break must be recognized or else the *origins* of the emotions we commonly feel go unidentified.

It is possible to have strong feelings in every conceivable direction—and most people do. Unless it is realized that a line of thought, even an unconscious one, produces a line of feeling, the sad result can be that the individual believes he or she is at heart a jealous person, an angry person, a sex-driven person, a depressed person, a free and independent spirit, or whatever else it may be at the moment and that there is no choice but to be "true" to that emotion.

You are often true to certain emotions in your dreams that you have no difficulty seeing as unrepresentative of your heart *once you awake.* A murderous rage is dismissed as easily as inordinate curiosity. And haven't you also *felt* yourself growing angry over just a fantasy about something that someone *might* do, an imagined slight that hasn't even occurred? This is a common mental activity that illustrates well the link between thought and emotion. The fact is that unless you have gained absolute mental discipline you entertain many thoughts that have behind them no deep conviction but are nevertheless capable of generating moods that are quite unhelpful to your relationship. And you can be sure that the parade of values set before you daily is causing you to feel certain specific ways that you do not seriously feel at all.

If some emotion is obviously disrupting your relationship, take the time to sit down and sort out your true feelings. Consult yourself deeply and often, because in your heart you are very gentle. If you are frequently swept up in the moods of the times and end up doing things that are not an aid to the friendship you wish to build, do not add to the difficulties by thinking you must also generate within yourself feelings of guilt and remorse. If you had seen the insides of as many marriages as Gayle and I have, you would not take the set of attitudes we have been discussing in this chapter so personally.

Guilt is not a practical emotion. While it occupies the mind there is no room for love, and this is true whether the attack is self-assumed or projected. Blame in any form is highly dividing. So if magazines suggest that honeymoon feelings can last, if talk shows encourage one to be angry and right, if TV dramas show that revenge and betrayal are justified, if newspapers picture breakups and attack as the normal course, if books tout the advantages of being single, and if songs romanticize sadness and loneliness, in what way are the modern couple to blame for undermining their own relationship? They are simply walking to the deafening beat they hear on all sides, and only in the sanctuary of their hearts will they find a little stillness and sanity.

Be more yourself and you will *truly* be different. Be more yourself and you will be more like your partner, whose heart is good. Pause frequently as you go through the day to listen for a moment to the sure, steady counsel of your sanity. Be one with a quiet knowing and not one with questions and longings and doubts. Forming a real relationship is hard because of how often efforts must be repeated, but it is not complex. It begins when just one person decides to be sincere.

CHAPTER II

Who Would It Take to Make Love Possible?

Letting Go of Romance

Being in love doesn't help. Not that it can be avoided. It's like a required childhood illness, a youthful and exotic headache that muddles the mind. She "screws up my memory and gives me gas,"[1] says the song. And if somehow it could be viewed in just this way, a temporary disorder like a coughing fit from some stray pollen, then at least the usual wad of inflated expectations would not have to be disposed of. As it is, friends are called to commiserate over each symptom of their passing until finally the last of the expectations is buried with great sadness and ceremony, like the pet cricket of a three-year-old, and is mourned, sometimes for years, as if an actual loss had occurred.

Who would cherish the thoughts one had during a coughing fit? And yet the momentary insanity with which we all begin these relationships is treated like a profound revelation or a set of mystical prophecies handed down from on high. Whatever

[1] © John Hartford Music.

you thought about your relationship while you were infatuated —what it meant, where it was going, what your partner was really like—you can now safely dismiss. Your relationship was never extraordinary, your partner was never above the crowd, and you have lost absolutely nothing in seeing this. Now you can get down to work, because what you truly want lies before you.

But try explaining all this to a couple who are about to get married. They smile patiently at you and then turn and pat each other on the knee. Gayle and I finally stopped taking this tack and just accepted that here, like all new couples, are two who think they are somehow different. We concentrate instead on giving them a few good shovels to dig their way out of the hole they will later find themselves in.

If you find yourself in a hole it is usually best just to sit in it peacefully before attempting to climb out. And as Gayle and I have witnessed so often, the expectations inherent in being in love can feel like a bottomless pit when they fail to materialize. So what does a couple do when the honeymoon is over and it is beginning to dawn on them that not only is their relationship not magical and wonderful, it has in fact not even begun to form?

They should not be discouraged. Above all, they should not blame each other. And in most cases they should not rush out and try to start another relationship with someone who has what this person lacks. Instead, they must begin a thorough housecleaning of their minds to free themselves of all they carry from the past. They want to work hard so that they can come together fresh, clean, open and willing to begin. In this sense their work is identical to the long-married couple who have decided to start their marriage anew and this time to get it right.

The Fiction of the Well-Matched Pair

The first piece of debris that most couples need to dispose of is the assumption that was behind their initial feelings of euphoria. In your case, I suspect that the feelings themselves have either vanished long ago or are beginning to, else you would not have picked up this book. Most couples who are still euphoric believe they have no need of instruction because they already have the relationship they want. This is merely the first manifestation of the assumption that will linger after all the romance has ended: They believe there are those who fit well right from the start.

Please take it straight from two marriage counselors: *There are no well-fitted couples,* at least not in the early stages of a relationship. This isn't to say that some do not clash less than others, for of course there are degrees of incompatibility. The kind of relationship you yearn for—and have a right to—is not the one you begin with but the one you will end up with.

Naturally the magazines and tabloids suggest otherwise. Here, displayed on the cover, is a couple who have everything —wealth, beauty, fame, sparkling personalities and a mutual love of stray dogs. And they found each other through the most remarkable set of circumstances! They rubbed fenders while staring at a hot air balloon and discovered they had the same insurance agent (insert of insurance agent smiling and saying, "I think it's just wonderful.") Naturally their ex-boyfriend, ex-girlfriend, and an arbitrary sampling of their children are not happy about the union, but this is mere sour grapes, because in every way they are obviously just perfect for each other. You can tell by their radiant complexions and their many self-confessed reformed ways. He no longer forgets to return calls, instead he forgets to honk during traffic jams, so content is he. And she has developed a sudden liking for the chili at Denny's. Before him, she would not frequent any restaurant that lacked hot finger towels.

Whether one reads the periodicals or not, the average person harbors the notion that these romances are as seen, even though most of them can barely last until the next issue. Consequently the same doubt festers in almost everyone of just what he or she has in the way of a partner. This person is in some way an inadequate or inferior starting point. Better to have waited for the chance of a lifetime.

The Road to Your One Great Love

Waiting for the right person to love is a very deep-seated and seemingly natural posture and is not confined to the married or might-as-well-be-married. Certainly no one is without relationships of some kind—a child, an animal, a parent, a business associate, a relative, a friend—and still the tendency is to wait. The future holds the key—perhaps at the next party, in the next town, with the next job, we will meet this ideal match and it will all be so easy, just like in the books, the movies, the songs. The ancient habit is to lean out of the moment into the one that has not yet arrived. But note that when one leans forward, one stumbles instead of strolls.

Can you remember as a child going to the park and just swinging back and forth, back and forth? Your eyes were closed. Or maybe you tilted your head back and stared up at the oscillating sky. So funny to see the whole sky move. You were happy. You had nothing else to do but swing.

It is not at all accurate to say you had nothing to worry about. Children's lives are just as vulnerable as adults! The dangers were not less, the potential decisions to be made were no fewer. What was different was that you had not yet learned that the future is a more practical and promising subject for your mind to focus on than the present. But is it?

Perhaps you recall riding your bike. Letting it coast down a hill. Maybe your dog ran beside you. You were not concerned with the cardiopulmonary benefits for either of you. The sun was at your back. The wind was in your face. You were in the present. So simple. But now these moments are a memory only.

We have lost the child's mind, that is all. We have buried it under a mountain of vain imaginings, and none is more vain than the belief that there are people who are better at love than we are, that love has pets and we are not one of them.

It is quite easy to waste a lifetime looking for the right circumstances in which to begin. If you will run your gaze over the many people you know and have known, perhaps you can see how universal is this dynamic. Everyone is trying to get past something. "My life will begin *when* . . ." When the kids get to sleep—when the kids go to college. When I'm over this flu—when I'm over this cancer. When the guests go home and I can be my myself—when the divorce is final and I will be free of you.

As we go through a typical day and find ourselves once again mired in some problem, we often have the feeling: this is never going to end. And we are right. It's just that we don't yet believe it. Thus we seek no alternative. Like a semi on an uphill grade, each event of the day is an annoyance that must be bypassed before we can mentally relax. And yet what happens? We pass it only to discover that we are behind a convoy.

Since "it" will never end, *you* must. Somehow you must learn a way to bring it all to rest today, this moment, this instant. And the road that leads to the one great love of your life is as endless as all the others. Even here you must learn how to stop passing people by. Your life will not begin when finally you have found "the right one for you." It will begin where you are. Someday, whoever is with you, it will begin.

When you were a child you did not let the fact that there were newer swings in more beautiful parks interfere with the fact that you were here, in this park, on this swing. You did not let comparisons to other bikes and other hills contaminate your enjoyment of this bike on this hill. And the same state of mind is now a possibility within your present relationship. So what if the bike, the swing, the spouse was *once* new? So what if you thought the two of you were somehow different from all the others? So what if your ex-spouse looks great in comparison, or your best friend seems to have done better than you? Decide now to let what is meaningless be meaningless. Take up what you have and walk. You have a partner and you have the present. That is enough to begin.

The Gentle Use of the Mind

What then will you do? You will remember—as best you can —the child's mind, the mind of acceptance and enjoyment. You will occupy yourself with whatever is the event or situation before you, and you will not hold back your heart from any activity. You will make each thing you do a gift to your relationship; thus you will think gently and not hurriedly and you will handle each possession, each task, each person with great respect and caring. You will let the day come to you rather than rushing to get to the day you want. Certainly you will plan and be organized and anticipate intelligently, but you will care for the future from the present and not from worry. You will do what you can do today and put tomorrow in the hands of tomorrow's peace.

As an aid to your way, perhaps you will have some simple thought to bring your mind back whenever you notice that it has wandered off into longings: yearnings for the old days, sadness that things have not worked out as you had hoped, regrets that you do not have the house, career, children, sex life you had always pictured, wishes that your partner was in some few ways different—ate differently, dressed differently, kept different hours, was less jealous, was more faithful, had greater earning potential, liked to get out more, loved children more, was less acquisitive, was more dependent, had different strengths, had different weaknesses, was different, was a different spouse. If a thought can take you from peace, a thought can bring you back. Its only qualifications are that it allows you to be more tolerant of the present and happier in the present. It should add a measure of kindness and permit you to better accept your partner the way he or she is. Any gentle thought can accomplish this.

Be certain you are clear that its purpose is not to trick the mind into believing what is untrue, but merely to act as a convenient means of interrupting the spiral of thoughts that leads to irritation, guilt, sadness, anxiety and other estranging and separating emotions. You might say to yourself, "I walk in gentleness." Stop the unhelpful line of thought at whatever point you catch it and begin silently repeating this sentence. Do not worry whether you honestly feel this way at first. You are merely affirming what you are on a deeper level and what you now wish to become throughout. Much time can be saved by assuming a mental position that for the moment seems only a potential and thinking *as if* the truth of the heart was your truth. Other possible ideas are: "My goal is peace." "My heart is at peace." "I know who I am." "I know where I am and I know what I am doing." "We are innocent." "We are one." "I am one with love." "I am one with peace." "I am undivided." Or some phrase you have always loved, or something that occurs to you at the moment. The words themselves are not important. Anything that comes from your heart will serve this good purpose.

When the mind concentrates gently on a single idea it returns to the present effortlessly, and whenever the mind is in the present it is, for the moment at least, free of the grievances of the past and fears of the future. Thus the relationship is freed along with it. These "breathers" can be very beneficial, so do not be concerned with how long you are able to sustain them. If you find that you quickly forget and once more begin drowning in the past, merely surface more frequently, like turning your head to inhale after each swimming stroke. The mind is trainable. It takes a while, but the effort, in its many possible forms, is a pleasant one indeed. It will lead you to a gentle relinquishment of all the misery-engendering thoughts of how the partner should be, of how the partner once was, that slowly crush the enjoyment and love out of so many relationships.

Because the chronic unhappiness of the world is now being felt by many people, there is indeed a widespread yearning for the contentment and peace that come from love. Yet so many of those who are willing to do the necessary work still believe that a *particular* body is needed, one with an appearance or personality other than those found in their present partner. It must be an interesting body, not dull and unsuccessful, of a certain age and weight. It must be open to speaking of important matters and it must enjoy doing so. It must be willing to attend the right events and read the right books and have heart-to-heart talks on cue. Or whatever other list of characteristics might be contained in the picture of what it would take to make love possible.

Seek not a special spouse. The ordinary spouse you have will do. Seek not a slim, nice-looking, passionate, well-informed lover. The reluctant, bumbling lover you have will do. Seek not even a loyal friend. You need only a typical friend, and typical is what you've got. So don't be fooled by packages. The heart of everyone is the same.

And if it turns out that your spouse is extremely attractive, inordinately wealthy, has great knowledge of the ancient Visigoths or especially long feet, accept this in good grace and look not down on the short-footed and unhistorical. Specialness is not to be sought or shunned; it is merely irrelevant to beginning a truly loving and peaceful relationship. Such a beginning starts today. And today you have been given.

CHAPTER III

Letting Go of Differences

The Old You Cannot Begin Anew

A true beginning implies that the old way has been vacated. If it has not, nothing *completely* new comes into being. A wedding ceremony certainly looks like a beginning, and yet within the mind of each participant the actual purpose is usually to vindicate how the individual has always been while at the same time lifting the clouds and "making the world go away." The marriage is entered into as a remedy, a correction of the past, but not as a personal correction. Each one has a separate list of ills that the other is somehow supposed to remove, but without calling into question his or her participation in those ills. Thus the whole orientation of most marriages and other "serious" relationships is toward the past. Nothing old is really left behind. Nothing new is really formed. And as time passes, the only thing that the couple knows with certainty is that the clouds are not being lifted and their personalities *are* being questioned.

In the first two chapters we spoke of the world's heightened awareness of its own unhappiness. The ancient sadness that was for so long pushed away can no longer be denied. Of course many, perhaps most, are still excitedly pursuing the same false hopes, but now there is a difference. The self-deception is not so deep as it once was because there is a growing sense of the outcome, that once they have acquired what they have now placed their dreams on, it will turn out to be "the same ol' same ol.' " And they are left not knowing what to do. Even withdrawing into personal depression and misery is starting to wear out its appeal. They have lost much of their faith in the old religions, the new psychologies, in position and wealth and limitless sex. They wonder where the current health craze is taking them—to be healthier than whom? To live longer for what? And so they panic and flail about, grasping at any straw, or settle into a stoical resignation and "keep on keeping on."

Although the world is now more aware of its condition and more skeptical of external solutions, it is clear that as yet there has been no genuine turning toward love. Relationships are still being looked at as something more to acquire, and a certain pride has developed in mere numbers. This approach feels like the self-betrayal it actually is, because no one can help noticing the litter. In our mindless rush from one relationship to another we are leaving behind a string of discarded friends, relatives, lovers and even children. And we know in our heart that each one was innocent and did not deserve to be misused. The attitude that spawns this waste must be questioned if we are ever to know love. So let us look at how a relationship can truly begin.

Trying to Match the Superficials

First, you must understand that there are many parts of you that cannot connect with anyone. And you must realize that you feel very protective of these parts. You feel attacked if they are pointed out and you have many memories of occasions on which this happened. You feel strong resistance when you try to let go of even one of these, and at present you have a number of reasons and excuses in place as to why you cannot make an adequate effort. Here, then, is the work before you—to let go of all the ways you contrast yourself, to shed everything you identify with that creates a difference, a gap, between you and your partner.

This is not the stupidly impossible task it may seem. It can actually be accomplished very quickly, but it probably won't be, and so recognize that if it takes time, you are willing to give that time because the end you seek will literally transform the world you live in and, in place of disillusionment, pour into your heart the sweet warmth that comes from loving and being loved.

What would it be like to pass one day without judgment, one day without questioning the motives or behavior of anyone? What would it be like to *welcome* the thought or sight of all people into your mind, even when you must say no or act contrary to their wishes? What would it be like to see, to actually see innocence everywhere you looked? Can you sense the connectedness and wholeness you would feel? Without your judgments, you would know love. It will not harm you to be a little confused, perhaps even a little anxious, but to be judgmental of your partner or anyone is absolutely and instantly destructive of your peace of mind. If you could walk through a single day without judging, you would know a world wrapped in light.

You must give up your judgments because they cannot join with another. Not only do most people not believe this, they proceed from the opposite position. They try to have contact with those who "have the same outlook on life" and who seem to agree with their opinions on additives, spiritual teachings, the weather, governmental practices, schools, the people down the street, and how awful the current flu is. Just listen carefully to any "normal" conversation. It is mostly a game of "I'll agree with your opinion if you'll agree with mine, and if by chance you don't, I'll reword it."

After the next conversation you have, pause and ask yourself if you truly believe what the other person said. Then ask if you even believe what you said. These little exchanges that pepper the day contain no real love or acceptance. Yet the answer is not, in the name of honesty, to become more specific and disagreeable. Literalism is no more true to you than conformity is true to others. Communication that is deeply satisfying does not take place on the level of words or behavior, although it may and should occur at the same time.

Our habit is to measure the quality of the relationship we find ourselves in by the degree that the other person agrees with our opinions, tastes and other personal differences. The one who agrees seems to "validate" us; the one who disagrees by saying so or by not displaying "common interests" seems to diminish us in our own eyes.

As a relationship proceeds, the partners may begin to lose their fear ("respect") of each other and show more signs of being at variance. To the egos of the individuals this will feel like not being loved, not being wanted, not being supported. And yet our views and preferences cannot *be* loved in any deep way. Having egos, we each see the world from a different perspective, and thus agreement on anything—the best children, the best kind of police, the best health measures, the best philosophy, the best landscaping practices—will always be superficial. Love does not take sides or refuse to take sides on anything. It is simply absent on this level of communication, and yet this level, if it is treated too carelessly, can block awareness of the love that exists, at least potentially, between two people.

Our minds are awash with loneliness and defensiveness and saturated with vague feelings of being distant from everything around us. This is precisely because we all try to join with each other by somehow getting our distinctions together. We can actually feel offended by a certain class of people or a certain class of behavior. We want so very much to find people who are like us and especially some one person who is exceedingly like us. But this will never happen except in those fleeting, isolated moments when we seem to "hit it off" with another person, moments which because of their intrinsic limits must deteriorate.

Most of us do feel a genuine bond with some individuals, and these few relationships are often peaceful and enduring. Note how absent they tend to be of strivings to wrangle and fake similarities. The dissimilarities are merely *accepted* and gently passed through. Hearts can unite despite differences, because on the deeper levels of the mind we are not interested in differences and the ego goes unheeded. We cannot think of ourselves as a collection of prized distinctions, be ever vigilant in watching over them, and have any hope of experiencing two minds at peace, two hearts beating as one.

Your List of Unjoinables

You need not relinquish your identity. There is no mad sacrifice entailed here. Merely begin questioning the many ways you have of defining yourself. Merely look more closely at your cherished list of unjoinables. Whenever you become defensive you are *not* questioning, you are not even looking. If you do not find some way of relaxing your self-image you will continue to long for a partner who is compatible with it, and the partner you have instead will react by wanting the same.

It isn't that you must stop being a finicky eater, a good conversationalist, a late riser, one who likes to fill out forms, who hates Democrats, who had a hard childhood or an astrologically superior birth. No changes in behavior are required, even though there are probably a few that would make life easier. What must change is your *investment* in being this bundle of peculiarities and wonders, because you simply cannot, for example, think it important that you are a person who chews politely without also judging your mate for munching like a horse. You cannot think it important that you are one who puts dirty underwear away and the toilet seat down without also judging your spouse as having the sensitivity of a dung beetle. Neither, if you are the horse-dung beetle of the household, are you free to add to the happiness and peace of your relationship by picking up your clothes and not picking your nose, if you cherish as part of your identity the *opinion* that these details are too trivial to bother yourself over. Love is neither a prude nor a nonprude, a slob nor a nonslob. The slob need not give in, neither need the prude. What *is* needed is for someone, and it matters not who, to commence examining what goes unquestioned as a sacred and untouchable part of his or her identity.

And how might that work be accomplished? First, it is necessary to be sure of the end you seek. You are not attempting to force changes of behavior in either yourself or your partner. That would merely lead to feelings of loss and resentment and would be added to the balance-due sheet so dear to us all. Your simple goal is to practice being your heart rather than your history. To accomplish this you must be able to distinguish between the two, and so you might begin by making a list, mental or, better still, written, of those characteristics that you believe distinguish you from others. It is true that they also divide you from others, but in many instances it might be difficult to see this effect at first. For example, you may think of yourself as outgoing and affable and might very naturally fail to see how these qualities could be separating. And it is quite true they are not. Nothing about your personality or habits is either promoting or defeating of love. What is separating is your *self-image* of being affable.

Specialness Must Be Defended

Whatever we think is true of ourselves that is not true of others we will assign importance, whether we like having the attribute or not. Even if we are at war with it and wish desperately to rid ourselves of it, we simply cannot identify with *anything* without believing it significant and feeling attacked when it is challenged. One who thinks of himself as outgoing will in his own mind single out those who are not, notice those who are, and be attentive to how this aspect of himself is received and treated. In short, he will think of himself apart, and will be apart, to the degree he thinks of himself as different. In the example of the amiable person, it is not the willingness to make overtures that separates but the mental appraisals and comparisons which accompany it. And these must be lessened for minds to join.

Do not be taken in by the notion that we love each other for our differences. We can like another's ego, and it is easier not to judge if we will see to it that we do, but liking is not the basis of love. In the song "Rudolph the Red-Nosed Reindeer," the other reindeer were suddenly flooded with love for Rudolph when he was chosen over them to lead Santa's sleigh. Do you really believe that? Well, Santa himself told me it was not so. "Hugh," he said, "that promotion caused so much yammering and head butting that I had to buy all the reindeer nose lanterns, and now they rotate."

It is possible to have unusual strengths or unusual weaknesses and still not call undue attention to oneself. The happy person acts out his faults modestly and is not flashy with talent. In a successful relationship each partner is caring of the other's ego and does not set it off by unnecessarily calling attention to differences. He who goes out of his way to contrast himself does indeed go out of his way. Even more important, real friends will instinctively guard their mental processes to see that lines of attack do not develop and that the universal tendency to look down on others' weaknesses does not take hold of their minds and create an undertone of judgment and disapproval.

The first line in the wedding vows that Gayle and I wrote for The Dispensable Church is: "I promise not to question your needs."[1] This is a mental more than a behavioral commitment. We all differ in the ways we are afraid, the ways we are dishonest, and so forth, and our habit is to think that our way is more reasonable. Is it truly more reasonable to be afraid of spiders than to be afraid of being laughed at? Is there really more deception involved in exaggerating when talking than in silently looking down on those who make less or have less? No one's inventory of his or her ego—if thoroughly made—could possibly reveal less insanity than any other ego. As has been said, we are equally insane (fearful, dishonest, self-absorbed, insensitive, etc.), it is only the ways we express it that differ, so in writing your personal characteristics list, do not unconsciously spin off rules and judgments as to how you should *really* be. Just be thorough and the lightness of your own peace and good perspective will begin seeping into your behavior almost unnoticed and will very gently make adjustments if adjustments are needed.

You of course will leave out many things, others you will overemphasize, and thus a follow-up step would be helpful. From this point on you might be very sensitive to any signs of bridling, of feeling slighted, of irritation, because defensiveness in whatever form is a tip-off that one of your self-identifying characteristics is being rubbed the wrong way, just as pride, fake modesty, or excitement signals that one of them is being stroked. There are ways you can be flattered and inflated and ways you cannot; there are ways to make you angry and ways that will have no effect; thus the people and circumstances of your day can be very useful in illuminating the boundaries of your self-image.

[1] 1. "[Name], I promise not to question your needs.
   I promise to seek your peace.
   I promise to put your happiness first.
   For it is in giving that I receive.
   And it is in helping you awake that I awake.
   [Name], I love you.
   I bless you.
   I want to walk home to God with you."

Being Un-different Together

Of even more help will be your thoughts of and contacts with your partner. Here you will see not only the ways you contrast yourself but the damaging effect each of these has on the friendship you are trying to build. Remember that during this early period of forming or reforming your relationship you are not attempting to dampen certain behaviors but merely seeking to lessen your ego involvement in them.

This is your time of watching rather than acting. You will discover an enormously effective resource in the process. To look at a problem and break it into its components slackens its hold on your mind, because the watcher in you resides in your heart. To watch without opinion is to watch *with* light—the light of sanity and love. Watching, if it is done properly, is a very gentle and healing activity: therefore be certain not to defeat its effects by monitoring and second-guessing yourself in some censorious and unhappy way. You simply wish to discover how you think of yourself, how you view yourself as apart from others, but not to change your individuality and definitely not to appraise and judge it.

In making this effort your partner—if he or she is willing—can join you in many practical ways. For instance, if you are both undertaking this project, you might encourage each other not to slip into self-criticism and not to begin little wars with your habits, but merely to list them or enlarge upon the descriptions you have already written. If some personality trait is particularly annoying and your partner wishes a form of self-correction, perhaps you could suggest specific ways of becoming more conscious that you suspect might be appealing, such as physically stopping and being very alert when some symptom appears, or your offering to stop also, or your partner carrying a notebook to record any thoughts or emotions connected with it whenever these are noticed.

It is perhaps best not to give your opinions of this trait or to point out those times when it is being acted out. If, say, your spouse believes that he or she is unable to say no to other people, it will *not* eradicate the apparent evidence and install a bright new self-image for you to argue that you do not see this inability, or that the inability is unimportant, or that it is really a manifestation of kindness. *The point is that your friend is distressed,* and whether he or she is right as to the causes or agrees with your ideas for solution is immaterial to your role as friend. So be a friend, one who works to lift the distress rather than one who tries to cast doubt on your mate's ability to perceive and reason.

In terms of the exercise that is being suggested in this chapter, you wish to offer ways to help with the looking and not with the analyzing. Possibly an offer to be available to step in and say no in your spouse's place would provide moments in which your partner could look more closely at what is occurring. Gayle and I often make phone calls for each other and give the excuses that the other would find difficult. The fact that one of us has this role more than the other is meaningless since strengths and weaknesses always balance out between friends.

Watching Without Judgment

Among many other traits (in some of which I still have strong investment), my self-image used to include being absent-minded. At first it was difficult for me to see how so innocuous a quality as this could cause feelings of estrangement between Gayle and me, especially when our friends, and even Gayle herself, seemed to delight in telling stories of my putting the mail in the refrigerator, or having gotten so absorbed in a conversation that I forgot to keep the accelerator down and was pulled over for slowness, or the time I drove to Safeway, came out with a case of Diet-Rite Cola, put it in the driver's seat, then climbed into the back. Why would anyone, aside from a traffic officer or psychiatrist, want to question so charming and endearing a trait as this?

John is usually very patient with me, and back in the days when absentmindedness was more of a problem, if I would fail to respond to a question or would answer inappropriately, he would merely repeat it until it finally got through. Jordan, however, having just entered the twos, was much more direct. He would repeat his request twice, and perhaps a third time at moose-level volume, and if that didn't bring me back he would walk over and slug me in the knee. The day I realized that my habit of not being all there needed looking into was the day Jordan aimed too high and, doubled up on the living room floor, I saw the light: Mental preoccupation was distressing my children.

I usually carry a little notebook in my back pocket—I call it my ego book—and whenever I am working on some newly unearthed mental miscarriage, as I frequently am, I do as we suggest often in this book and record any passing thoughts or feelings that seem associated with the problem. In the weeks following this incident the entries I made showed that many others were being made unhappy by this trait and also revealed another effect, that these times were not withdrawals into great ideas but into a merry-go-round of inane and often cruel mental chatter that was not serving my life purpose of becoming a more loving and forgiving individual. In what way was it loving to misplace things that my family needed, or not to be fully present when Gayle wanted someone to talk to, or for her later to realize I had not heard what she had been telling me? In what way was it loving to scare my family by driving in an unconscious way or to waste time woolgathering when we needed to leave for an important event? In what way was it forgiving to let my mind slip into idle thoughts about other people? All living things should be thought of carefully, not carelessly.

These are just a few of the consequences that surfaced in my notes, and by seeing the extent of the unhappiness caused by this seemingly innocuous little trait, I became motivated to practice being conscious. Whenever there was time—and there is always time for what we want most—I would stop if I realized I was musing and would write down anything I was aware of: emotions (frequently feelings of being distant and apart), the thoughts themselves (often wordy and hard but not impossible to get at), the surrounding circumstances (commonly ones I would want to escape in some way), my physical actions (usually ineffectual if a task was involved or self-negligent if I was, say, eating). If I did not catch myself during an episode but only realized what had happened afterward, I would stop at that time and record what I could see in retrospect, which was sometimes helpful in new ways. For example, I might see that this time the idle thinking was brought on not so much by boring or demanding circumstances as by some compliment received or some piece of ego-gratifying news— which of course did not gratify at all but merely launched me into a flurry of thoughts about the future.

I knew better than to fight myself through self-reprimand, or by struggling to listen, or by trying to be in the present in some tense way. The approach that saves time, as with any difficulty, is to become more conscious of the problem itself and more conscious of the happiness and other benefits of the moments that are free of it. Watching is not a form of preoccupation because it entails inner stillness. One merely sees what one can see. It is like being very quiet in the presence of a little wild creature that one has caught sight of.

Triggering Sadness—Triggering Peace

There is of course no neat end to the step we are suggesting in this chapter. You will not suddenly find yourself without a self-image, without ego investment in your many strengths and weaknesses, but perhaps you can sense how it is possible to steadily lessen this investment and how doing so would gradually free you to join hearts with your partner. To hold our dissimilarities with another sharply in mind triggers a very old and profound misconception: that we are not fully understood and accepted by anyone and that although we can temporarily deceive ourselves into thinking otherwise, nothing in heaven or earth will ever alter this fact. There is a level of experience to which this perception applies and is wholly accurate. The error comes in believing it is the only level.

Self-images cannot match because they are outgrowths of individual histories, and the division between them is far more absolute than is commonly realized. In forming acquaintances, people are constantly mistaking superficial similarities for deep joining. Within long-term relationships the disparities, repeatedly seen and yet still thought meaningful, are not as easily overlooked. Even a hint of disagreement can end a recently gained sense of unity and confirm our ancient conviction that we are solitary.

Throughout the day little differences surface in seemingly minor discussions of what to buy for dinner, how to treat the child's cough, where to set the air conditioning thermostat, whom to invite over to see the vacation pictures. Couples do not understand why these conversations are distressing and why they so often lead to flare-ups or to miserable little silences. They conclude that the disparities should not be there and that something is very wrong with the relationship. After all, with so-and-so at the office this does not happen.

It does not happen of course because so-and-so cannot be pinned as the sole source of one's unhappiness, as can one's spouse. Furthermore, so-and-so's goodwill is needed, whereas one's spouse's is not, and so naturally there is more of a show of agreement and more self-deception that agreement is occurring. The little stabs of aloneness are overlooked and go unattributed, and the notion continues that one is freer to be oneself around so-and-so, who is an altogether more pleasant, deeper and happier individual and is in fact a true friend, unlike the hopelessly unamenable person back home. Thus the age-old story repeats itself without the new relationship or the old ever once moving past the level of ego compatibility.

Your armor must become less specific and defined in order for your heart to shine through. You need not overhaul your personality. This would merely make your defenses turn in new directions, but your identification with your own self-definition must weaken to the point that you now have something to offer that is truly compatible. Whether your partner likes opera or bowling, prefers an early or late bedtime, values cleanliness or is a free spirit, yells or is stoical, goes to a different church or no church, burps or is tight-lipped, wants kids or only gerbils, is amorous or self-sufficient can give you no indication of the depth of love that awaits you.

So when you make your list of unjoinables, be certain to include your opinions and beliefs because these too are part of your self-image. Then begin the gentle and happy work of loosening your grip on the ways you must think and be at all costs, for it is indeed costing you your prospects for love. Every time you watch rather than react you become a little less well defined and thus freer to be something more, something deeper.

Use a calm, judgment-free watching as your means of correction. Look at what just happened but make no rules. Look at what you are doing now but launch not into battle. Merely notice, merely observe, and watch too the softening of old behavior patterns that accompanies such an indirect and enjoyable approach.

Your partner is your personal opportunity to be at peace. Nothing less. And certainly there is nothing more. Whatever he or she professes or does, this one potential remains invulnerable. You have before you an ongoing occasion for sinking into your own gentleness and expanding. So let this be your choice. Let your partner stimulate an ease reaction, let his or her face, whether seen or thought of, be your signal to shed the weight of your cherished rights and step into grandeur. Your other choice, the one that this world has exercised to the point of devastation, is for you to continue a hard defense of the ways you are different. To be whole or to be right—that is the decision you will make this instant, and in every instant that stretches before you.

CHAPTER IV

Which Relatio
Are You In?

well-being of
blindly tha
necessar
center
idea

The Center Path

No one truly wishes to be unhappy, and since a lack of commitment is always the decision to be unhappy, it is clear that most couples are profoundly confused as to where their interests lie. They have a few tiny areas where commitment seems essential, and a vast desert where it does not. Many people are quite consistent in "working out" daily and in staying well informed. But these are little commitments that cannot make up for a lack of commitment within one's being. A *great* commitment will extend to all aspects of one's life. If you are wholly devoted to your partner, this devotion will naturally spread to your children, employees, etc.

We carry with us an old fear, an insanity really, that love is as finite as motor oil or money and that the amount given to one person depletes by that much the amount available for another. Consequently we think we are continually being forced to choose between our friends and our spouse, our career and our home life, the well-being of our child and the

our marriage, and we act out this assumption so
t indeed our life seems an endless series of sad but
y choices. It has never occurred to most people that a
path, a happy medium, is possible, even though that
is given occasional lip service.

The ego side of us detests happy mediums as deeply as it
disbelieves in kindness. Love is so foreign to the part of us that
wants to be special that it can imagine it to be anything it
chooses, and it chooses to consider love a scarcity that must be
used selfishly if there is to be any left over for itself. Thus in
our confusion of inner and outer reality we believe that love
always demands sacrifice. When friends are over for the evening, the children must not interrupt. When work remains
unfinished at the office, we must be distracted and preoccupied
at dinner. When sexual problems arise, we must long for the
old lover who did it right.

If somehow we could learn to focus on the relationship at
hand and give to it the best part of us without fear that this
part will diminish in the giving, if somehow we could experience the increase in happiness that comes from exercising happiness, then there would be true balance in our lives and one
person or activity would not threaten the time and place of
another, for we would know this is not necessary.

The cruel idea that all things must compete can be raised to
doubt by any couple who sets out to prove that harmony is
more natural than chaos. The child does not have to be either
neglected or turned into a tyrant. One's job does not have to be
jeopardized by domestic problems, neither is one's only option
for peace to seek refuge in work. And the ties one has with old
friends do not in fact demand insensitivity to one's spouse.
Sanity is always a possibility and comes naturally to the mind
that decides to be centered in what it is doing now and flexible
about what comes next.

Love Is Always Like Itself

A friend of ours gave us permission to tell the following story. Much to the relief of his family, he has grown to be quite unlike his old self, but what he did one day back in his early thirties exemplifies the chaotic effects of the belief that there are different kinds of love each in competition with the other.

Unlike Gayle and me, this couple had their first child very early in their marriage, so early, in fact, that the husband in many ways was still in shock over the loss of his single-life routine, one component of which was never to miss seeing the Sunday-afternoon reruns of "Kung Fu." He had managed to salvage this one practice, which was a cherished symbol of how his life should be.

One weekend he, his wife and four-year-old daughter had walked to a nearby park and spent a couple of hours so peacefully and enjoyably that he had remarked that he couldn't understand why he had looked down so on family life all those years after college. As frequently happens when one recognizes that one has been made deeply happy by kindness, his ego reacted. Suddenly he looked at his watch. It was seven minutes until "Kung Fu," and this was the episode he had missed seeing time and again.

Young children do not understand being rushed and do not like it, and so by the time he had snatched up his daughter and the three of them had run home, she was shrieking to all the world about the perfidy of parents who would promise a little child one try at the monkey bars and then not deliver.

The front door was locked and so they ran to the back and discovered there that no one had brought the keys. There was, however, a doggy door for Knucklehead, their basset hound.

Our friend commanded his daughter to scrunch through and open the lock. She protested that she had been told repeatedly not to use Knucklehead's door. But this was an emergency, her father said, and added that she was never to do it again. Perhaps remembering the injustice of the monkey bars, she decided that the time had come to take a stand for what was right, and she flatly refused. Our friend, realizing that it was now one minute into the hour, picked her up and pushed her through.

More shrieking. Attempts to crawl back out. More protests about parents who misuse little children. But finally it became clear that she was too short to reach the dead bolt.

At this point her father told her to stand back and, as his wife and daughter watched in stunned silence, he kicked in the door and went straight to the TV.

For about a month afterward he had a noticeable limp, an increased deposit was requested by the landlord, and his daughter had to be patiently reinstructed in the concept that animal doors are different from people doors. Even more damaging, of course, was the lingering doubt he had planted in his wife's and daughter's minds—that he was a stranger, one who could not be relied on.

The Inherited Way of Looking

By shifting his focus to another relationship, in this case his old bachelor relationship with himself, our friend did indeed become a stranger to his family, albeit for hours only. Even if it is not spoken or acted out, just one thought that places another relationship above the primary one can engender a mood of estrangement completely destructive of the sense of oneness the couple may be experiencing. It is seldom understood just how fragile is an atmosphere of gentleness and connectedness. It cannot be betrayed by even a momentary wavering without disturbing results. The ego layer of our mind is a continuous offering of such thoughts, most of which go unreceived in any deep way. But from time to time we allow our attention to become immersed in some sad or exciting consideration that holds no love of the present, and the instant we do so real communication with the person before us is blocked, even though we try to appear the same.

If you privately stop feeling at one with your partner, regardless of how virtuous the reasons, it is impossible for this mental pollution not to spread. One of the ways, and perhaps the deepest and most pervasive, that couples stay on the verge of a genuine relationship without ever beginning to experience it is to view each other through the eyes of their parents. Very few couples believe they are doing this, and yet it has been our experience that there is virtually none who do not. Chapter VII will go into more detail about the specific effects of childhood conditioning, but let us first examine the most obvious consequences of remaining in the old relationship we had with our parents.

All parents teach a *way of looking* to their child even as their parents did with them. This naturally includes specific attitudes toward men and women. These are not necessarily found in what parents *say* to the child, because often their attempts to instruct come at times when they are feeling judgmental and entail concepts that they themselves have not mastered. One of my dad's favorite refrains was, "Always look ahead," which was possibly the one thing he most consistently failed to do (especially when driving).

Coupled with the usual meaninglessness of most intentional teaching is the frequently overlooked fact that children, especially in their most formative stage, instinctively give attitudes far more weight than words. Very young children are extremely sensitive to what a parent is feeling moment by moment and what general subject he or she is afraid of or longs for or is judgmental of, because this is, within their little world, the very mood of the gods, and their happiness and even their safety depend on reading it accurately. Parents believe they can mask their basic attitude, but this is simply not possible with a young child, whose entire reality revolves around it.

As they grow older, children begin to deceive themselves in

the same way as the parent by believing they can change their
outlook merely by changing their behavior. Most adolescents
think that by dressing differently, speaking differently, chal-
lenging rules, and so forth they are freeing themselves from
their past. What they fail to recognize is that they are still
controlled by their parents' way of looking whether they ad-
here to it or react against it. Then as teenagers become young
adults, they believe their renunciation of the past is complete
because now they have earned a higher or more up-to-date
degree, embraced a different occupation, and have chosen as
their partner another "type" of spouse. Yet none of the basic
inherited attitudes has actually given way to the deeper urges
of the heart merely because of a few shifts in externals. In a
sense our ego is given to us, and it protects itself by counseling
a preoccupation with appearances.

Seeing Naturally

Do not let it concern you that you believe your spouse is like
or unlike one of your parents. In either case your way of looking at a spouse remains the same until you can distinguish the
layers of your mind and identify with your natural core of
beliefs and feelings. If it is still possible for you suddenly to
find yourself judgmental or anxious, you may be sure that you
continue to take personally the feeling tone that once ema-
nated from your parents.

I acted out my father's gut feeling that women will always
desert you by having (after one early marriage) a single long-
term spouse who I, until recent years, was afraid to give myself
to wholly. And I thought myself superior to him because he
had multiple wives. No fundamental change occurred until I
identified the components of this deeply ingrained attitude toward women and took up the considerable work needed to
replace them with my natural sanity.

By no means are all inherited ways of looking out of rhythm
with one's core. There are many areas of mental freedom in

every parent's life. Perhaps your mother had a natural sense of playfulness and fun that would surface, say, during car rides with the family, or your father had an easy honesty in business dealings with other men. My dad was always very kind to toll booth operators, service station attendants, and others in service roles and to strangers in general. My mother saw great humor in animals and was instinctively a friend to them. And naturally I could cite many other strengths they both possessed. The possible varieties of happy, loving attitudes are far greater than the ego's repertoire of pettinesses, and certainly one's parent should never be viewed as a dark source of damage. One remains psychologically damaged only so long as one chooses to, even though the motivation for choosing again may be slow in coming. You wish to commence the process of shedding an old and dead skin, to peel your eyes, as is the saying, so that with you every last family tradition of misery can end and you can see the relationship you are in with soft and receiving eyes. One method of making such an effort will be presented in Chapter VII, but before a step like that can be undertaken it is best to first recognize the overlaying dynamic that plagues so many relationships.

Comparisons Hold No Kindness

Specifically, you must come to see that it is wholly without meaning whether you suspect that your companion is in many ways like or has many qualities in opposition to those of your parents. Neither interpretation gives you any insight into this person's heart, and it is this and not your partner's pre-formed personality or genetically received appearance that you can unite with in love.

We are asking you to become acutely aware of this very common train of thought and deliberately to doubt its relevance. Along with the deformalization of conventional disciplines such as physics, medicine, psychology and psychiatry has come a popular need to show oneself brilliant and original in all fields. Thus many people now believe they are gaining ground by analyzing their partner in whatever terms are current, reasoning out connections they do not see, and convincing themselves and others of therapeutic and even mystical concepts they basically do not believe. At present it is obviously very chic to be able to explain one's current relationship and what one intends to do about it in terms of stunning insights into the past of one's partner. There is usually much pretense in this and very little kindness. Kindness requires no more than the willingness to see like a child, to see as if for the first time. Any comparisons you make of your spouse to your parents, whether they are positive or negative, will blind you to ways of immediate aid and healing, and if on no other grounds than this they can reasonably be dismissed as mere mental static.

One fact will become increasingly clear as you begin to experience a real relationship: All hearts are one; all egos are separate. It is the latter half of this insight that will allow you to question the import of similarities or dissimilarities between your parent and partner. Egos, if they are nothing else, are different. They live on the blood of their differences and without them they fade. Thus you can be certain that your partner has neither the counterpart nor the converse of any quality your parents possessed. In large measure each person's ego is a subdivision of his or her parents' egos, and it can be quite helpful to trace back its origins. Categorizing one person as "like" another person's parents is not part of this process and must always be inaccurate because it is judgmental.

Seeing One Who Is Not There

This does not mean that similarities cannot be *seen,* but they cannot be seen in depth. People are in fact attracted to or shy away from what they perceive as parental likenesses in appearance, life-style, disposition, and other trappings, but even though they believe that their choice of a spouse was made on these grounds, and other important people in their life concur in this view, this does not make the view accurate or, more important, prove that the marriage was therefore mistaken.

In the course of giving long-term counseling Gayle and I have repeatedly discovered that there were far sounder and sometimes quite touching reasons for a couple to be drawn to each other than either of them was aware of at the time, and it is our opinion that at the root of most decisions to form a permanent relationship is a very pure and wise desire, regardless of the ego involvement that of necessity accompanies it.

Even if, say, a man thinks that he is intentionally choosing "a girl just like the girl who married dear ol' Dad," this level of his decision is so superficial that he may eventually see through it *in general,* and yet continue to believe that it is possible for there to be true duplication among egos—or true foils—in the area of specific qualities.

For example, perhaps your mother liked to go out and your wife likes to stay home. Look a little deeper and you will see that there are a thousand reasons and ten thousand ways to go out and to stay home. Look a little deeper and you will see that there are no true opposites among personalities, just differences. Perhaps your father was anger dominated and so too is your husband, and perhaps all the men in your life have been anger dominated and you wonder if your choice of a spouse was neurotic. Please believe us that this is one worry you need no longer have. Your way of looking at anger may indeed be a problem, but anger itself is not a limited edition. It is not a 1920s Coke bottle or a Calvin Klein dump truck that you either have or don't have. Anyone with an ego has anger, and there are as many ways of interpreting it as there are people with points of view. You have locked yourself out of your partner's heart by turning this person into Frankenstein's patchwork monster or the relics of a saint if you persist in classifying him or her as another individual of another time whose function in your life was to play another role.

If you can become aware of these little thoughts that stab

your friendship and of their utter arbitrariness, then you can step away from the patterns that play themselves out, often for a lifetime: A woman finally is forced to admit that her husband is not the man her father was. However, in a world this large there is bound to be someone who is, and so, regretfully, the search must continue. A man suddenly realizes that although he didn't think so when he first met her, this person is really just like his mother and though the mistake is his there's nothing to be done for it but to push her away as a freak, just as he has had to do with all the others.

Be alert also to the smaller injuries, the momentary turnoffs that these same loveless comparisons can create. You do *not* see your mother in this person's social instincts, sexual interests or taste in birthday presents. You do *not* see your father in this individual's drinking pattern, reading habits or way with cats. If it is a good comparison it will turn on you. If it is not, then you already may sense how separating the thought is. See the person, not your past. Lift the veil of comparisons from your eyes and love simply and directly.

No One Is Unable to Commit

Although their parental relationship is the one that couples most commonly superimpose on the present, the image of many other faces can mask the face of their companion, resulting in similar blocks to communication. We have mentioned the demands of old friends, comparisons with former lovers, and contending commitments to work, but of course the potential list of relationships that can be confused with the primary one is long indeed: contacts with an ex-spouse, the call of a committee to meet, visits from relatives, the coming into town of a spiritual teacher, phone calls from grown children, or merely insistent memories of another person or group who seem to "demand" comparison. Whether the conflict appears to be overt or purely mental, the issue is still one of commitment.

Genuinely commit to one relationship and all the others will come into perspective. This statement does not have to be believed before it can be practiced. Commitment is a moment-to-moment decision rather than sentiments about the future. Since it can only be exercised in the present it is within anyone's grasp, and no person lives who cannot commit and who does not commit to something many times in the course of a day. For most the choices are conflicted and no theme but confusion can be seen running through. Such mental habits cannot provide the secure substructure needed for real friendship to develop. And yet the mind *can* exercise a straight line of dedication in place of an unstable and shifting one.

If you cannot commit to your relationship for a year, commit to it for a day or a week, and during that time think of nothing else, long for nothing else, in other words, be honest. When the period is over, sit down and consider deeply your heart's decision. A real friendship can be knitted one stitch at a time as well as cut from whole cloth. If it would help you stay focused to write this out in contract form, to specify the term, and to say in detail what committing yourself means to you, then do so. Your ego will argue that a single purpose demands more effort (meaning more pain) than multiple aims, but nothing is lost by seeing for yourself that this is not true.

A Relationship Cannot Give

Is there less rest in a stable relationship than a conflicted one? Is there truly more freedom or more possibility of freedom when partners are left to fend for themselves? To what exactly does your ego wish to escape? Please do not be frightened of this question. There is an insane argument spinning within the minds of most couples that their relationship *should* be giving them . . . what?

An ideal sex life? But what is an ideal sex life? A house and financial stability? Do you know anyone whose house remains good enough and whose financial condition is accepted? Someone who can be a father? Look at the men who have "enough" children. Someone who can bear you children? Look at the women whose families are "complete." Are they happier because of this magic number of bodies? Or perhaps you want no more than someone who appreciates a good book, supports community chamber music, and can on occasion interact intelligently with a few interesting friends. Do you believe this is *now* what they want who have it?

A garden of discontent grows in the hearts of most couples, and it will thrive and spread only because it is not honestly examined. Again, if it would help, write down your thoughts. Pluck each grievance from your mind and scrutinize it as you leave for work, prepare for sleep, read a magazine, hear a song. What is this bed of weeds composed of that is smothering the hopes and good intentions you both began with? See it in its entirety and you will *be* committed.

Most people long for an affect rather than a real relationship. They want to be overwhelmed with some vague set of sensations which the other person is magically supposed to supply. They want romance and exciting common pursuits, or a certain infusing quality to life, or a feeling of support from which to launch their high-minded quests, or a sense of safety and a strong shoulder to lean on. They want everything except to give. To give is belittling, thwarting, boring and nonactualizing—and what would one say to one's friends? To give is to opt out and miss out. To give is to give in. To give is death. But to seek and never find is life.

Below the Sentence Level of the Mind

You will begin to free yourself from this insanity once you decide on the form your efforts will take to become personally acquainted with your mind. Essentially, there are only two levels. One is dominated by words. The other is immersed in peace. One is in search of an experience. The other is already having it.

You wish to become increasingly conscious of the level that begins and ends little sentences. Practice awareness of these so that the images and feelings they generate will not overwhelm you and toss you around like the trash of an alley caught in meaningless swirls of wind. When the wordy layer of your mind proceeds unobserved, as it does unrelentingly with most people, you cannot be yourself; you will be merely different but alone. Begin to notice, and you will simultaneously start to sink below pettiness into a very happy and gentle inner stillness. The sentences will continue but you will fail to get caught up in them as easily. You will still be aware of the chatter and what direction it is heading at the moment, but you will feel no compulsion to take its meaning to heart, for you will recognize that these are just the many conflicting voices of your past, agreeing on nothing, fearing and judging everything, and that you are something more, something whole and sane.

This still and deeply happy area of your mind is incapable of being pulled back and forth between friends and spouse, job and children, church and marriage. It is free of *questions* of which relationship comes first because it is profoundly interested in the present. It sees where its most peaceful course lies because it looks at decisions quietly. This is a power you can exercise. It will harm no one. A peaceful decision may not be greeted with glee by everyone concerned, but it will not truly injure. However, before you can employ a power such as this you must be in possession of the part of your mind where it dwells.

Identify, then, those thoughts that keep you swimming in smallness. Do you have an unspoken bond with your parents to look down on your spouse? Do you respond to your child's requests in a way that you know will create still another issue in your marriage? In your humor do you side with the guest against your partner? Are calls for your time outside the home met more quickly than those from within? Some unregarded sentence in the mind shows you the way to each of these mistakes and a thousand more. Awareness and peace walk easily around each one.

You might begin by setting aside a quiet period each day for sentence watching and continue it until the practice begins to transfer to other moments. This could be supplemented by your carrying a pad and writing what you can notice, or saying the thoughts out loud, so that with your whole attention you can begin to grasp the full dimensions of the nonsense. Do not fight your mind, of course; just observe it.

The success of your primary relationship is up to you. Therefore seek the help and goodwill of your partner so you do not fail. To practice together is more effective than practicing alone, but if practice alone you must, this will be infinitely more effective than spite. If you choose peace for yourself, you choose it also for your partner. But if you choose merely to be right, your own sadness and betrayal are doubled because they are shared.

Begin at the Ending Point

Everything you have done in life has led you to this point. Are you now going to deny this point by not committing yourself to it? Do you not see that you must forgive the events of your life if they have brought you here? Otherwise you do not know where *here* is, because it has grown out of causes you still deny. Is it not possible that for you to be where you are now is good?

There are no coincidences, and although you do not find yourself with this person by accident, are you truly *with* this person? Or are you still living on speculation and misgiving? Is there some large block of you wondering if things did not perhaps get off course and you are now the one thing out of place in the universe?

To give yourself credit for some degree of inner knowing does not mean you must stay forever in the same neighborhood, driving the same car, and never change your underwear.

It does not mean you will remain with this person. But here you are. You have not lived a mistake-free life, but how will you ever know that where you are now is a mistake unless you first commit yourself to it? If you have not yet committed, you have not yet *had* a relationship, so how can you decide against it? Unless you give all your heart and all your attention to something, to anything, how can you see it?

So many people are *not* going to leave their partner but they *are* going to wonder if they should for the rest of their lives. Consequently, they will have no real life.

You have nothing to lose but your feeling of meaninglessness, this impression of a life that is scattered and directionless, this sense of things never having come together. What *must* come together is the heart. Do not be half-hearted, only half in your relationship, only half in your house, your job, your body, your car, your children. Commit to what you have and where you are. Commitment has nothing to do with tomorrow. It is no more than walking through today with purpose and clarity. Remember that the world has forever waited for the right circumstances in which to begin. Do you want to be a loving, gentle, kind person? Then your partner is your work. Do you truly want to learn forgiveness? Then whom can you forgive more completely than your partner?

It is an all too old and sad story that in their last days most people turn to look back on their lives and with profound regret see all the opportunities they missed to show kindness and to make their loved ones happier. Suddenly it is obvious what their priorities should have been, and they are bewildered that they could have spent so many years in blind pursuit of trivial and wholly meaningless accomplishments, that they touched so many lives and added not one thing of value to any of them.

This need not be your story. For you *will* look back. And you will see honestly what you may be pretending to be quite confused about now. Instead of waiting until it is truly too late, you could have such a moment now. Stand back from your life and see it as it is at present. Picture yourself on your deathbed with nothing else to do but look. Continue this long enough to consider and receive one simple idea: that you know precisely how to balance your life. You know how to hold a job and be fair to the people you work with, how to be a good friend to old friends and new, how to be a real parent, and at the same time how to let your partner see that you are present, you are there, one who accepts and appreciates, one who does not judge, and especially one who listens to no clock and has no notion of what it could possibly mean to be too devoted.

You will not magically have an increase in intelligence when your time of dying draws near. Whatever you will see then, you can see now. You *have* made the decision to join with one other living being, and so naturally love must begin at the starting point you have chosen. You have said, and you truly meant it, that you take this person's hand to walk through life, through all it brings, together, that together your strength is great, that together you will bless the world. And there can be no doubt that the world needs your example of love. So give it freely, because herein lies your personal happiness also.

Love begins with your chosen partner and then flows gently outward to your children, your parents, your friends, and all other living things. Conflict and competition are no more a part of love than they are of sunlight or rain. Like a fountain, love must begin; like a waterfall, it must continue. So of course you put your partner's happiness first—there is only one happiness. How could your children know love if their mother and father have none? There is only one love, one kindness. How could you touch the lives of your employer or colleagues in the gentle way you wish if your very house and resting place contains no peace? There is only one ease, one rest, one peace of mind.

And this is what you will see in your final days, or now, whichever you choose. During this holy instant you will confuse yourself no longer with concepts of one love for parent, another for spouse, one for the oldest child, another for the youngest, one for your art, and one for your marriage. As you look in quiet release of all the future's clamoring, you will know that love is love, and either you put love first or you fail to do so.

The Parts of Your Relationship

INTRODUCTION

In the children's stories that we and our parents grew up hearing and in the movies and songs of just a few decades past, what followed marriage was so agreed on by all that it did not have to be stated or shown. Mere wedding bells or the cry of a newborn baby was enough to suggest all the rest. In most fairy tales when the man and woman finally came together they were, by that act alone, rendered enormous power to be happy. We know from the story line that they did not have this power before, but in forming a union they were invested with some mystical force that gave them dominion over misery forever.

And once upon a time we believed that the everyday story should be very much the same. Love, we thought, is physical recognition. It is known by the face or figure that triggers the right sensations within. And if it is mutual, as it always is when it is "true," it will do all that is needed by itself, ironing out like a giant steam press the silly little peccadilloes in groom or bride that might otherwise have ruffled absolute bliss.

But of course we no longer believe these childish fantasies. For we have kissed the prince and he turned into a frog. The princess was discovered to be a witch in disguise. We see through the self-delusion of our forebears, and like a teenager, we have broken the grip of our past through change, change and more change. We change our body, our name, our career, our hair, and over and over we change our relationships. The good times last only so long, and we must synchronize the breakups accordingly. We have learned to go for the "best" of life wherever it may lie and whatever strictures there once were against it. "It doesn't get any better than this," the beer commercials assure us, as they picture a brave new world in which no one is obliged to be with the same person twice.

The secret that every marriage counselor knows is that although new-age adults abandon relationships as if they no longer held any of the old meaning, inwardly they still believe the myth that to unite the right bodies calls down the blessing of the gods. They fantasize as much as ever about how it will be when they, too, find the person who will make it all happen. Their only question is how to get rid of the wrong one so that they can get back to searching for the right one. It is true that love solves all problems, but clearly this is not love.

Love allows us to forgive, to let go of the past, to unstop each gentle current of the self. But it does not reform. It will not make our partner into the idol of our fantasies or home us in on the individual we deserve instead. Love is felt in our heart and it treats the heart of our partner benevolently. It seeks no external evidence for its existence, no confirmation in another body's behavior.

What is thought of as love, what is described in the lyrics of songs and displayed on the quivering lips of soap opera stars, is a very misty and immature view and has little to do with "being good at relationships." Such an expertise *does* exist, but it is learned. It begins with an effort, because the mind must choose to turn from selfishness in each of its specific allures. No battle is required, but concentration is needed to see the decision through.

Love—to the degree we are capable of it—is not enough. People who truly love each other break up all the time. The population as a whole is remarkably unimpressed with the *skills* of relating. In learning to ski, one does not fling oneself wishfully down the mountain. But in forming relationships people *do* fling themselves and are always surprised at where they land.

In Section II we center on the specific strengths that *no* one is born with, the ones that must be acquired, and also on the state of mind that begins to develop when a couple has made a sustained effort.

Once you learn to be of help specifically, you gradually become one who could not do otherwise. Then the means and devices of concentration will be redundant. Once you have learned to take each other seriously, you will see no difference between you, and help and happiness will be given and received without decision. Then will it be true that "all you need is love," because to need any other attitude will have become unthinkable.

CHAPTER V

Freeing the Relationship From Its Past

The Effort to Appear Normal

In the last chapter we discussed how parents try to shield their attitudes from their children but do not change the attitudes themselves and end up teaching both the attitudes and the lesson that they should be disguised. The best liars first deceive themselves, and in our desire not to seem like the only ones who can't catch on to how relationships work, we have all become consummate liars. There is an unconscious pact among most partners to present a united front that they too have what all who live together are supposed to have. How many times have you and I been surprised by the breakup of a relationship we thought was sound? Why just last week the pair was cooing and giggling like mating turkeys. Now they will speak to each other only through an accountant.

It isn't that a couple should keep the world posted on every cross word that passes between them, or even be conscious at all of the veracity of the image they are presenting. It is that more effort goes into shielding those who don't matter than in

being kind to the one who does. Most people are deeply cour-
teous to strangers and persistently careless with their own
partner. While attempting to prove the viability of our new
doctrine that any imperfect relationship was a mistake from
the beginning, that our partner exists at our whim and is there
merely as an experiment in magic, we too are caught off guard
by affairs, sudden ultimatums, secret visits to the attorney, or
suggestions of counseling. Who needs counseling? Our relationship is better than most! "Oh Lord it's hard to be humble
when you're perfect in every way," sings Mac Davis, and it
unquestionably requires humility to seek counseling or in any
other meaningful way to admit that "things are not working
out."

Things are meant to work out. This is the attitude that has
not changed despite trial marriages, open marriages and eulo-
gies on freedom from marriage. Our secret mental life is essentially the same. We daydream of "getting someone" and we
watch the dramas and read the magazines that pretend this is
possible. But still no real thought is given to how to join one's
life with another. Somehow we shouldn't have to concern ourselves with this. Somehow there should be someone who will
live happily with us just as we are without any study and
application, without any genuine sustained effort on our part.
Somehow life should be different.

But why should life be different?

Why should two who value separateness not have trouble,
and a lot of it, trying to practice oneness? Why should two
who value change, by their mere decision to live together, suddenly see their changelessness? Unless you have chosen a saint,
your partner is going to change. It is not realistic to expect
that any human will remain the same in the course of a permanent relationship. You too will change. And this will cause
differences between you. Issues will arise and probably there
will be some long unhappy periods that must be weathered.
But if you persist, there also will come discernible progress
toward real friendship and a gradual increase in peace. Out-

ward changes in tastes, interests and pursuits can become as unaffecting as shifting cloud cover or the cycles of leaves. What is different in you cannot join and will always change, but what is alike in you can join with what is alike in your companion, for the heart reaches heaven and cannot separate from Love.

The decision for a permanent relationship is the decision to see the storms through that *will* arise. Of course one can think of extreme situations that should not be endured, but even children perceive that most separations need not occur. There is no deep reason for it other than a couple's belief that they could do better and have a right to do better, that the world should be different for them. But of course the world never ends up being different.

Are we saying then that all who wish a long-term relationship should surrender to a twilight zone of dwindling hopes and resign themselves to ending each day feeling overburdened and unsupported, saddled with a mate who will not see and will not try, and deprived of every bright moment so commonplace in the life of all young Americans who drink beer? Yes, we are saying your alternative is either this or to end your life alone with no less pain and remorse than the thousands who will end their lives in this manner today—unless you are willing to look at the world as it is and then to turn radically to the simple answer your heart holds out. Because surely it is clear by now that being married brings no more freedom than being single. The world *cannot* be different for you, but you can be different within it simply by choosing to work. And if you work, your relationship will gradually transform, regardless of how reciprocal you believe your partner's efforts to be.

What Is Unforgivable?

All issues spring from discontent. The less discontent, the fewer issues. Discontent can be dealt with directly, but this is so inclusive a goal for most couples that the more restricted approach of learning how to release their minds of the specific grievances that have accumulated is generally more productive. However, if the underlying problem can be kept in mind and a growing atmosphere of acceptance can be valued, then the techniques for letting go of old issues will be more quickly applied and have broader effects.

Most couples begin their relationship with genuine goodwill and see quite well the goodness that the other has at heart. As time passes, disagreements come but do not entirely go, and to these are added a periodic act or neglect that takes on the dimensions of an outrage in the mind of one of the partners. This person cannot forget what has happened, and his or her unwillingness to forgive becomes an issue in the mind of the other partner equally as grave and may even seem to provide justification for a repeated offense. Thus the grievances, large and small, slowly mount, the partners grow further apart, until at last they seem to have almost nothing in common and no real reason to try to come back together. What they had in the beginning is looked back on as mutual deception, or the mere perceptions of immaturity, and what they see in each other now as reality. They find the thought of a deep union with this person repulsive and would rather keep their means of staying at a distance intact or end the relationship altogether than try to understand. They think that if they forgive they will have to spend more time together and it is already bad enough. Can this marriage be saved? Many magazine articles and newspaper advice columns, not to mention well-meaning friends, proffer solutions to this question.

Willy has five girls by a previous marriage and Tilly is a hopeless pinball freak. The girls don't like pinball, they like video, and besides, Willy never brings home enough quarters. Should Tilly have an affair to cure her of her obviously Freudian fixation with plungers? Or should the girls be sent to foster homes?

No, you are so wrong. All turned out well when Tilly was

given a Brittany spaniel on Memorial Day and the girls were paid in loose change to walk it daily.

There are of course many good ideas in magazines and the like, yet very often the problems and solutions are stated in terms of circumstance and behavior. It is Gayle's and my experience that although some relief can on occasion come from a change in the outward situation, the deep joining we are speaking of in this book is only attained by a permanent shift in attitude, and that once this begins to occur, whether the couple's external lot in life improves or deteriorates will affect very little the peaceful place they now increasingly occupy in each other's heart.

In early 1980 we joined with another couple to begin a group in Santa Fe for parents whose children had died. There is no more horrible circumstance for a couple to find themselves in than this, and if events could destroy a marriage, certainly it would be enough. Yet we have known many couples through the years who responded to their child's death in a way that gave them great unity and strength, and we have also known many who used the tragedy to turn against each other.

Nothing is more confusing than the suffering and death of a baby or little child, and the opportunities for mutual blame are enormous. But blame is never justified because it is never what is called for, and if this can be seen in the extreme of a death, it can also be seen in cases of affairs, excessive drinking, violent fights, extravagance or stinginess, overburdening sexual demands or little sexual interest, fastidiousness or slovenliness, humorlessness or shallowness, and changes in religions or political beliefs. Once again this implies nothing about the advisability of continuing to live with someone; it is simply a statement of fact that there are no unforgivable traits nor has anything taken place between the two of you that cannot be successfully released from your minds.

For several years Gayle and I also worked with battered women and rape victims, and in some of these cases a change in the person's life situation was necessary. But regardless of what changes were made, forgiveness was essential to the healing of emotional damage, and this is equally true of the accumulated anger and discouragement in any long-term relationship.

How Many Alterations Does Your Partner Need?

The most common approach to solving issues permanently is to "learn to live with it" or, if referring to the matter does not cause too great a flare-up, to make periodic bitter little asides. Neither tactic ends the mental skirmishing, nor does it usually stop the behavior that has been singled out. The toothpaste is not squeezed from the bottom, one spouse still exaggerates when telling others what something cost, socks continue to be put in the laundry wrong side out, one partner constantly interrupts, or the first of every month toenail clippings are found in the bed.

More than once we have heard individuals cite one of the foregoing as the primary reason they walked out, walking out supposedly being the ultimate permanent solution. Although they may have believed this was the cause, obviously no one could be so narrow-minded as to focus on the location of a clipped toenail and discount everything else. Nevertheless, these kinds of issues can grow to surprising dimensions because they become symbols of each other's lack of concern. At first one partner notices that the other eats with his or her mouth open but thinks little of it; a few years later that person is bolting from the table whenever it happens. The offending party believes the issue so petty as to be undeserving of attention and therefore frequently "forgets."

In the next chapter we will suggest a method of reaching agreement on how circumstances and behavior should be changed, but this procedure requires your partner's cooperation and this you may not get for a long time. Still you can be happy. Still you can continue contributing to real friendship.

We return to the principal concept of this book: that the key to your relationship lies in your mind and not in changing your partner. It's not that your partner couldn't stand a little changing, but perhaps you are already beginning to see the conflicted results that trying to force this can bring. And once you have your victory and your days are filled with right-side-out socks and properly squeezed toothpaste, will you be happy with your partner? Not if you still believe that what your body's eyes see can make you unhappy, because soon you will notice this person's habit of not cleaning the spoon before dipping it into the mayonnaise and a growing tendency to doze off just before reaching climax.

In everyone's journey the time must come when the searching stops and happiness begins. This starting point is reached with the realization, or the suspicion, at least, that our mind is more powerful than circumstances. It is true that we allow ourselves to be made miserable by the most amazingly insignificant happenings, but when we *"put our mind to it,"* even in the grossly undisciplined states that most minds are in, we can remain ourselves under remarkably trying circumstances.

Very few burst into tears or slip into a murderous rage while in the dentist's chair. And yet the melodrama of the mouth will never end. You didn't like having your teeth brushed when you were two and you won't like having dentures when you are eighty-two, and in between are more years of dental appointments than years of marriage. You have been in this chair before, you are in it now, and you will be in it again. You have merely *"set your mind"* to getting through the appointment, and you do, with surprising equanimity and politeness.

This is the outcome because (1) it was your decision to go and so you climbed onto the chair with relatively little conflict, (2) you concentrated on remaining stable (centered), and (3) you forgave the situation and people involved and did not carry any deep grudge with you when you left. Is the way your spouse slurps soup truly worse than having a needle jabbed into your cheek or a drill descend into your nerve tissue?

If you *"have a mind to"* you can endure whatever your spouse does with the same equanimity and politeness and afterward allow what happened in the past to remain in the past. But you will not do this unless you *"enter with a will."* And these four expressions, so common that they are clichés, show how thoroughly familiar every person is with the process.

Rather than letting one or more of these outrages continue to be outrageous, if your partner is not tractable, then sit down by yourself and decide what kind of person you are and how you will remain yourself during any future episodes of your partner's behavior. Perhaps picture in detail the way your spouse might act and imagine equally as vividly your ability to be one who is understanding, one who is a friend, one who has a mind and is not just a set of trite reactions.

Your Preoccupations Transform You

This book can be used jointly or by yourself alone, and as you may have noticed, we speak to the reader sometimes as two people and other times as one. Naturally, to decide together on an approach to building togetherness will facilitate your goal, but this is not yet a realistic expectation in most relationships. The ego likes to pick its own books, therapists and TV shows, because the ego, above all, prizes separateness.

Gayle and I now do most of our therapeutic and spiritual practices together. In the morning we set our inner purpose for the day together, we let go of the day together at night, and together we pause frequently to regain our perspective during the day. But this was not our procedure for most of our relationship. Gayle went to a Jungian analyst and I toyed with various spiritual and psychological teachings until about fifteen years into our marriage, at which time we started devising our own joint self-improvement program. The separate work we did brought us to the point that joint efforts were possible, but if at least one of us had not first made gains individually, we would probably not be married today.

If there is a great deal of unhappiness in your relationship, you must decide whether you wish to go down with the ship—even if you *are* angry. Be aware of the urge to sacrifice what you can have in the name of what you cannot. It may be necessary for you to carry this relationship by yourself for a very long time. This was Gayle's role in the early years of our marriage because of the lack of respect for one's partner I was taught by virtually every member of my family, step-relatives as well as relatives, most of whom have been married at least three times. Gayle did not leave; neither did she sink to the level of my conditioning. She knew that waiting for me was as good a laboratory to work in as searching for another, and so she waited and worked on herself.

Nothing is accomplished by living under one roof with the same body year after year. Neither is there gain in switching bodies. Nor in living alone. Appearances are not as important as your mental state, which remains unchanged for as long as *any* external circumstance preoccupies you.

We are free to look at the world through any lens we wish. Those whose preoccupation is money view all things in terms of what they cost, of how something might be used to gain more, of what loss might come, of what others have or do not have. If the preoccupation is with sex, the person notices sexual nuances everywhere. Each look and gesture, each physique and piece of apparel, each billboard and periodical is seen in the light of its sexual significance to the individual. Those engrossed in health scan their bodies for sensations and symptoms. They look at air, food, clothing and all their surroundings in terms of how it might affect them. They think and talk health.

Many fixations are possible and for most they shift: now to personality, now to their appearance, to possessions, to danger, to intelligence, to relationships, and so forth depending on a multitude of external triggers. The only preoccupation that is not stimulated and fed by surroundings is a preoccupation with the peaceful realm of the self in which love can be found.

And it is this you lose access to if you count your relationship a disaster and become one yourself by answering attack with attack, pettiness with pettiness, judgment with judgment. For being right is also a preoccupation, and it converts the world you live in to a single subject as unfailingly as a fixation with health or money.

How Hard Does Your Partner Work to Torment You?

Perhaps you begin most days in a fairly good state of mind but then something happens and a slight downward spiral begins. More often than not it may seem to you that your partner is the cause of the problem and that if it were not for how this person usually behaves, you would be more consistently happy.

It is unlikely that your partner's goal in life is to sabotage your happiness. He or she may be quite inventive, but except in horror stories, most people are simply too selfish to take the time to torture another individual every day. Yet you may *feel* as if this person goes out of the way to make life hard for you. As a first step, please see that no one is that consistently perverse. There must be some other factor besides the utter iniquity of your partner.

The mistake most individuals make is to reason backward from their bad mood to the bad motivation of their spouse. The ego thinks that unhappiness is always externally produced, and since one's spouse is the most convenient external, he or she is assumed to be the cause. But in relationships the ego does not stop there. If a cloud rains on our picnic, we have no animosity toward the cloud, but if our spirits are dampened because our mate is not exciting enough, we conclude that this person *could* be more exciting if he or she would only try. We see the lack of effort as an attack on us and never stop to question if this is even the cause of our unhappiness.

You will not know love and oneness as long as you attribute your partner's behavior to shabby motives. There are two intents for every act and you must learn to overlook the first in preference of the second. Honor the gesture of heart behind the behavior. This is not a complicated task.

Merely pause and ask yourself what you believe is this person's deepest motivation. It is safe to assume that your partner tries hard, that your partner wants to be happy. And surely all individuals think of themselves as good in some way. Why do you need to add darkness to this seed of purity? For when you do so you merely shift your gaze to their selfishness and cherish it above their self. Do not lovingly dwell on every unhappy possibility as if this person's mistakes were the only ones in the relationship. Very consciously and very deliberately feel the basic goodness of your partner, and know the reason you choose to do so.

We can easily go a lifetime operating under the most unlikely of premises because we have not carefully examined the background arguments in our mind. Identifying the causes of marital unhappiness has been Gayle's and my primary work for several years now, and we have seen that most people go through the day thinking that their spouse has put them in the mood they are in, and so naturally suspicions over the spouse's motives become their primary focus.

Despite its falsity, the premise takes root that our partner is hard at work devising new means to make us wretched, retaining, of course, a few ongoing ways because of the obviously splendid results. Again and again our attention is drawn to what he or she is up to *now,* and thus we fail to discover what empowers these actions to affect us. If the action were the cause, we would be made to feel a certain way consistently, whereas in reality the same behavior can evoke any number of positive and negative reactions.

Let us take the example of the spouse who occasionally comes in late from work. Does this create the same emotion in his or her partner with each instance? No, because the one who is at home must react *from* a state. Even on the most superficial level it can be seen that if that person is running late on dinner, or has a neighbor over visiting, or is in the middle of a TV program, or is expecting the guests to arrive any instant or, say, has someone at the door who could be dangerous to the late-arriving spouse, the real reaction on each occasion would probably be markedly varied even though he or she might pretend to be angry as usual.

The simple truth is that our ego is inconsistent in its emotions and not as controlled by others as it likes to seem, yet we have at any time the option of not deferring to these feelings, whatever they may be. To exercise this choice we have to become aware of the factor within us that generates our erratic moods so that we can distinguish between it and our source of unvarying feelings. This factor is always a thought that enters the mind prior to the triggering event. When it is made conscious and dismissed, the mind simultaneously regains its ability to love.

How Poison Enters the Mind

This interpretation of the cause of relationship-disturbing emotions is difficult to believe at first and may need to be worked with on a sustained basis before it will be seen as a reliable and very friendly fact. Anger, fear and judgment are protected by the belief that they are externally produced, and yet once your experience begins to cast doubt on this assumption, the power to be happy can develop quite rapidly.

At some point in the day, and perhaps earlier than might be expected, you accept as fact a little thought that wanders into the mind. Instead of passing through uneventfully like most of the others, this idea is held on to and its meaning is accepted and believed. Now it becomes like a slow-acting poison taken into the mouth. While it remains in your system it infects every aspect of you and your relationship. It sets a mood and then you react from that mood, and your partner reacts back. You are dealing here with a very normal human pattern and one that is almost unconscious.

The tipoff that you have taken an unnatural thought to heart is that you will eventually feel anxious, irritated or judgmental over something that happens. Whenever any of these three basic ego components is present, you can be sure that no matter when you accepted it, the generating thought is in the background and can still be detected.

Your function is somewhat like that of the archaeologist who sees signs of a buried past. You wish to commence immediate excavation and this you do by sifting through every thought you are aware of until you find the one that set your mood.

Say it is morning and you and your husband are at the bathroom sink doing the aesthetic procedures to face and hair that distinguish humans from the lower beings. But you notice that your mate seems not to comprehend that the calling for art and beauty is as strongly felt in you as in him, or else this person ironically believes he has better materials to work with —because he has positioned himself at the center of the mirror, leaving you only the merest edge, which sunders the canvas of your face, not to mention your heart.

The inspiring words of your high school field hockey coach come to mind. "When your opponent steps between you and the puck, a misplaced foot can be quite effective."

"Why did you do that, dear? All you had to do was ask me to move over."

Evidently you have hurt your opponent's sense of fair play more than his toes, because he has still not relinquished his position. However, since this is a bathroom, not a hockey field, you will reason with him.

"Why should I have to ask you to move over? A, you can see me standing here. B, you know my ride comes before yours. And C, it is as much my mirror as it is yours."

"Yes, dear, but it is entirely my foot."

Although he has shuffled around a little, his upper body is still leaning into the central and dominating position. The inspiring words of your high school basketball coach come to mind. "When an opponent is between you and the ball, a misplaced elbow can be quite effective."

Now his upper body is leaning entirely if somewhat noisily out of view. The mirror is yours for the taking. And as you step before it, you can hear the lovers of art and beauty everywhere applauding wildly.

Here it would seem that the mirror-hogging husband is the cause of the wife's retaliatory feelings. However, if you were the wife you would wish to take a moment to quietly review what happened. In the course of looking back over the morning you might be able to discover an instant prior to entering the bathroom in which you accepted a thought that left your mind prone to seeking retaliation. Some other thought would have predisposed it to depression, righteousness, sadness, peevishness—over the same incident. When an ego idea finds a resting place in the mind it establishes a state very much like eating a certain type of food establishes a state in the stomach. What comes next hits this preexisting state, and the result is a specific variety of upset.

As the wife in this example, you must at least accept on faith that your partner's actions did not directly cause your desire to get back, even though they did trigger it. If at the time you entered the bathroom your mind had been dominated by a deeper and more natural thought, you might have responded to the same behavior playfully, humorously or peacefully. Yet what happened instead?

Reflecting back, you recall that when you woke you looked at the clock and realized that you had less time to get ready than usual—but that accompanying this simple recognition of a fact was a thought of, let us say, fear. Your husband did not wake you when you had asked him to and it occurred to you that if you were unable to get ready in time the car pool might leave without you and jeopardize your job. Here was evidence that your husband is not reliable. It is not safe living with him. And other scenes of his unreliability flashed through your mind.

The precise form that the thought took is unimportant, and you need not remember anything about the moment except that fear entered your mind and you accepted it as a reasonable characterization of reality that you then lived with. You got out of bed in fear, dressed in fear, ate breakfast in fear, and finally went to the bathroom mirror in fear, where the fear then took form. The apparent reason was that your spouse seemed to be delaying you again, but remember, if you had not been carrying the same anxiety for an hour or more—if you had not been walking through the day unconsciously—you could have seen many peaceful ways of getting mirror space.

Seeing the Blocks to Happiness

Whatever your ego tells you is not true. Anger, fear and judgment are always groundless, and in almost every instance they can be relinquished. Certainly conditions could be so severe that very few people could avoid an ego reaction. If you woke with a potentially deadly bark scorpion crawling up your leg, as I did one night, you would probably be frightened, and yet we have a friend in the forest service who knows exactly how to pick them up and does so frequently, and this person would not be afraid. Fear was not inevitable; it was a product of my past experience with insects plus the confused mental state of an abrupt awakening, and perhaps if I had not panicked I would not have been stung.

Most of the daily occurrences that couples become upset over are not flagrant provocations, and the individuals truly do have the option of a deeper response. To begin to exercise this reliably several steps must be taken, the first of which is to catch the upset too late, but to catch it nonetheless.

Often couples believe this stage continues longer than it should and they become discouraged and dive back into their old unconscious way of relating. But if the alternative to trying is the usual loveless muddling, why not try?

Do not even *expect* to lessen the degree or number of negative feelings at first. Simply practice looking through the thoughts in your mind for signs of recent disturbance. Detecting little upsets, even those that suddenly occur when your partner is merely thought of, will furnish excellent practice.

Episodes of separateness often can be recognized more readily in retrospect when the passing of a few moments has allowed the mind to become less defensive. There is a remarkable tendency within relationships to deny that anything out of the ordinary has happened or to sweep it under consciousness by thinking that a little unhappiness from time to time is normal.

We do not like to see unhappiness plainly because we believe that true discord indicates that our relationship was a mistake from the start. But if this were true it would call into question every union since time began. Moments of unhappiness are so frequent as to be the essence of most relationships, and yet unhappiness is not "normal" and does not have to be accepted and endured. Thus the importance of becoming highly sensitive to the momentary moods of estrangement as well as the grand eruptions. Of course "sensitive to" does not mean "judgmental of." You will always stop seeing accurately when your mind shifts into attack.

Recording the Blocks to Happiness

An effective way to practice would be to schedule a short period each day for reviewing the previous hours. For instance, if one of the partners leaves in the morning, the one who stays behind could write down any less-than-peaceful, less-than-happy states of mind that he or she has passed through since waking.

If you are the one doing this you might begin by describing how you feel now that your partner has left and then proceed back through the morning, identifying any moods that you can plainly see are not conducive to good relations, for example:

"I feel faintly elevated now that I have the house to myself.

The thought seems to be, 'This is how life should be.' And the thought of [name] coming back this evening is a little dark and heavy. There is an image of [name] asking if something is finished rather than greeting me.

"As I continue back, I see that my thought as [name] was leaving was one of anxiety, but I can't quite get at what the fear was about. However, the feeling before that when we were discussing everything the mechanic needs to be told about the car was definitely one of resentment. I remember thinking, 'This trip would not be necessary if you had bought the car I suggested.' "

And so forth, back to the time of waking and lying in bed. A more abbreviated description or simply a list of feelings and thoughts could be made instead.

If there were incidences of friction or upset, even in a minor form, then try to detect what condition your mind was in prior to exhibiting the separating emotion and what thought might have produced it. The producing thought need not be deeply analyzed or even finely described. At this stage you wish merely to get in as much practice at this new form of detective work as possible. Two or three weeks should begin to give you a sense of the dynamics of the unhappy outbreaks between you and your partner.

If you are the one who leaves in the morning, a similar period of recounting should be held as soon as you have a quiet moment. If it is possible to do this out loud or only silently while driving to work, then this would be better than waiting until much later when some of the morning thoughts have faded. Again, if there was an incident between you and your spouse, attempt to track down the thought you had accepted before that which made you prone to react the way you did. A written record can be very useful in identifying patterns, and perhaps this could be made covering a period occurring during the evening (your thoughts about coming home; your first reaction to seeing your partner; etc.) and on days off.

Alerting Yourself to the Blocks to Happiness

The first or recording stage of practice involved identifying the predisposing thoughts after they occurred but before they faded from the mind. If you are conscientious, by the end of this first stage you will be aware of certain thoughts that set you up for trouble which before you did not even know you were thinking. The concentrated attention you will devote to these during the second stage will begin to give you proficiency in what you will come to see as a highly freeing discipline. This is not to say you will shortly be beyond the influence of all such thoughts, for that is the work of many years, but you will now have the *option* to dismiss the onset of misery, whereas before you had none.

There is no limit to the means one can use to be more conscious of the specific ideas that set anger, judgment and fear in control of the mind. The mere desire to do so, if it is heartfelt and persistent, is sufficient, but often we tend to waver when dealing with something so cherished as our own ego and can well use a device or two to give us focus. The aid you choose should be simple, because your goal is immediate and uncomplicated. You merely want a way of knowing when your mind has just embarked on a dangerous course.

To this end we would like to suggest a few procedures we have used ourselves and found quite effective. The first is an imagery in which you picture an alarm system, lightweight and comfortable, placed on your head. It monitors your thoughts and when it detects any that are fearful, judgmental or angry an alarm of your choice (bell, siren, police whistle, flashing red light, etc.) will come on. To turn it off all you need do is interrupt the idea. If later, even only a few seconds later, you begin thinking along the same lines, the bell (or whatever other signal you have set it to give) will sound again, and again your only function is to *not* complete the thought.

If you would like to have it installed now, sit in a chair and be as quiet and still as if you were listening for Santa Claus. And just as it did when you were a child, the present will come to you without your ever seeing who delivers it.

Feel it being gently positioned on your head. . . .

Now it is ready.

To test it you merely set it for the signal you want and then think any of the three kinds of thoughts that attack your relationship. Instantly the alarm goes off.

Being a device that is controlled entirely by your mind, should you persist in not listening to its alarm, it will obey your wishes and shut down. Therefore, if you realize you have gone for a long period without being alerted, merely turn the system back on by wishing it so.

Some people prefer not to use a formal imagery game, and for those the repeated effort of making their mind sensitive to the coming of these thoughts might be all that is needed. If they would like to imagine an alarm going off when one of these becomes conscious, that much might be added.

Examining the Blocks to Happiness

As you continue to give this form of support to your relationship, doing no more than declining to finish loveless thoughts, you will begin to notice recurring mental themes. These may concern an old grievance against your partner, some recent unsettling argument between you, or maybe a general but familiar feeling of dislike or irritation with as yet no discernible idea behind it. For example, in keeping your daily record of attack thoughts, you may discover that very often you look forward to being with your partner at the end of the day but that this mood gives way to a specific darkness within moments of seeing your partner, regardless of how he or she behaves.

Obviously these more persistent thoughts need special attention. Perhaps you could set your alarm system to give off a different or louder signal when one of these occurs.

Or as part of your morning preparation, you could take in turn each of the recurring ideas you have become aware of so far and say, "When I realize I am thinking about this I will stop and look at the thought."

The more closely you look at an attack thought, the weaker its hold on your mind becomes. The grounds for anger and judgment are insane yet so obscure that a logical necessity for these moods is at first presumed. You do not *have* to react negatively instead of intelligently to anything, and it is never in your best interests to do so. Your ego divides best interests the way it divides love and argues that it is possible for a reaction to hurt your relationship and yet serve you. Do not doubt that you have accepted this confused reasoning whenever you turn against your partner.

Closer attention is therefore your first response to a recurring thought. You may even recognize it as basic ego nonsense but if you have not yet familiarized yourself with all aspects of it, do not attempt to dismiss it, because if it is done too quickly this can be a form of denial that pushes the idea from sight, where it seems to take on a life of its own. Freeze it right where it is when you catch yourself thinking it. Look at it carefully. And *then* allow your mind to proceed in gentler directions.

Gayle and I have observed that it is often a single thought, dwelled on half consciously for years, that gradually drains all hope and life from a relationship. Something happens or fails to develop that dashes a major expectation. There was an affair. A chronic drinking problem developed. The family never moved to the country. The couple could not have children. The sex life soured. And because of this dark turn in destiny, the relationship has been defeated—in the opinion of one of the partners. And usually both partners have their elected development to explain why the relationship is now a washout. And yet thousands of couples have put these and many other so-called crushing blows behind them. A blow continues to crush only because of the darkness enshrined in one person's mind.

Be alert to the argument that to look closely at your negative thoughts will make *you* more negative—"I don't like to dwell on negativity; I'm a positive person." If the negativity were outside of you this might be valid, but it is your negativity, and how could becoming more aware of the ways you sabotage your own happiness possibly hurt you? When any thought of fear or attack is given rein to roam the mind, you can be sure your sphere of influence is darkened.

Stand quietly or sit down and surround the thought in stillness. Do not ask yourself what it means or how you will ever be rid of it; in other words, add nothing to the thought. Merely see it as is. Some of it will be murky but will grow clearer as you examine it, especially if you limit your mental activity to description and do not drift into analysis and comparison. Judge neither the thought, yourself for having it, nor the people it concerns. Look at it the way a baby looks at a cockroach: with complete intensity and innocence. The next time the thought comes around, scrutinize it once again, and continue this until nothing about it surprises you. If you wish to keep a record of each new aspect you discover, this could speed the process.

Discarding the Blocks to Happiness

Once you feel confident that you know this thought quite well, you can safely begin eliminating it from your experience. If it is a scene from the past, you might take in turn every person and object in the picture that keeps coming to mind and surround each one in light. The ego does not like light and if it realizes that by handing you this memory all it will get from you is light it will quickly desist. After you have done this on one, two or at most three occasions, a shorter version should be used in which you surround only the principle figures, your aim from this point on being merely to have in place a short, peaceful response to this unhappy offering.

If you prefer a verbal approach, your initial mental treatments could be to consider in turn each thing you see within the recurring memory and say,

"That is merely a rug. Rugs are innocent."

"That is merely a city. Cities are innocent."

"That is merely a letter. Letters are innocent (or paper is innocent, ink is innocent, envelopes are innocent)."

"That is merely a chair. Chairs are innocent."

"That is merely a face. Faces are innocent (or hair is innocent, chins are innocent, eyes are innocent)."

After one or two applications you again wish to come up with a shorter form for future use so that your mind-clearing technique does not become tedious. Thus when the thought recurs you might say, "I have no more use for this thought. As a gift to our relationship, I will not pursue it."

In identifying and alerting yourself to the various ideas that precede upsets, the other category of thought that you will be dealing with is anticipations and judgments about the future. This can be a more deceptive area since it concerns what has not yet happened and therefore can appear to be one-of-a-kind ideas rather than recurring ones. But it will become increasingly apparent to you that you think about the future in the same *ways*, regardless of the uniqueness of upcoming events. Because the future is not yet here it must be imagined, and we each exercise surprisingly little variety in how we do this.

The core of us, the place where stillness and peace reside, never becomes preoccupied with the future. It is therefore our ego that is behind these thoughts, and when they are examined closely they are seen as still another version of fear, anger and judgment. Your aim is to dismiss the disrupting way you view the future and not the future itself. To go through the day being prepared promotes peace and strengthens your relationship. Yet note that very few thoughts about the future prepare you for anything. They are merely another way of practicing being miserable—depressed, anxious, scattered, excited, discontent, ill—humored. Unless there is a decision to be made about a step that can be taken today, treat the thoughts you have about the future the same as those concerning the past and see if you cannot loosen your grip on them.

Very often, as in the example of the mirror-hogging husband, the disrupting thought will contain both past and future elements (i.e., judgmentally selected scenes of the husband's past unreliability, fearful pictures of the car pool's future reaction). If your attitude toward some upcoming circumstance is a familiar one—"Soon the housework must be started (so I will be depressed now)." "Not long before I can crawl into bed (so I will feel delayed and interrupted now)." "Soon the bill will come in (so I will be anxious now)." "Not long before we leave on vacation (so I will have my heart in nothing I do now)"—then break it down into its separate parts as much as is needed to give you a sense of thoroughness and, as with the memories, surround each person and object in light or verbally declare their innocence—("Those are just dishes. Dishes are innocent." "Those are just the children wanting a nighttime story. Children are innocent. Stories are innocent.")—until you feel the charge that this particular attitude has for you begin to dissipate. Of course, if there is something you can *do* about the future concern (e.g., call the company to determine how many days after billing payment is due; preselect a story you would enjoy reading out loud), then do not fail to act. As we have stressed before, simple overt acts affect the *mind* more quickly than purely mental means and should, whenever feasible, be the first step to restoring inner balance.

Many other techniques are possible for releasing recurring thoughts, a number of which we have covered in *Notes on How to Live in the World . . . and Still Be Happy*. We do not go into more detail here because the object of this book is not to present a general approach to life but to focus on ideas that have been helpful to couples, and the practice of seeing innocently is the specific remedy indicated in long-term relationships.

The Source of Freedom

Naturally there is more to freeing your relationship from its past than identifying, examining and releasing the specific thoughts that are generating ego reactions. There was a past before the relationship that also must be released. However, the strength and happiness of the friendship you are building can be greatly enhanced merely through an increased awareness of current thought patterns. It is even possible to accomplish all the work that needs to be done through this means alone, because as long as awareness is exercised, it will continue to expand and will eventually reach all disturbed areas of the mind. Nevertheless, Westerners do not have generations of this form of meditation behind them and for most there are additional means that can save time, one of which we will discuss in Chapter VII.

The power of your thoughts to make or break your relationship cannot be overstated. We are so used to proceeding as if all cause and effect were confined to what our eyes can see that if we find ourselves unhappy, our mind begins dwelling on this as proof of our partner's culpability. How many sound but not perfect relationships have crumbled under the weight of this erroneous premise! Gayle and I know of one divorce that was precipitated by the wife's failure to bring home a head of lettuce. And yet we know of another marriage that grew in strength after the husband neglected to cover a hole into which the couple's one-year-old fell and drowned.

A great deal of work must be done before you can see with complete honesty that your partner cannot *make* you unhappy. Yet, as you may already know, your thoughts about your partner can become the most punishing of hells. The aim of your efforts is not to prevent breakup. Neither is it to start a war with your mind. Rather it is to begin looking for solutions where most people never think to look—in one's personal commitment to peace and gentleness. Nothing your friend does can thwart such a commitment because it is not based on behavior or circumstance. *Love does not have to be honored or even received to continue being love.* You can be the kind of person you wish because your state of mind, and therefore your happiness and your power to bless, is within your control. But good intentions will continue to slip from your grasp until you see the link between idle thoughts and how you feel. This you *can* see, whether the means you choose are to write your thoughts down, say them out loud, schedule periods to stand aside and watch them, imagine hearing them broadcast, picture them appearing on a screen, or, as we have done, set an alarm to go off every fifteen minutes or so to catch them. The determining factor will be how deep your desire for a real relationship is and how unwilling you are to defer it.

So begin this gentle and happy work today. Let the effort rather than your partner's acknowledgment be your reward. Allow not the past of the relationship to continue as a dark force within your mind. Allow not even a shadow to be cast on your joy. Make of your mind a friend. Begin today to have the kind of mind you want, free of what is over and done, free of the same tired old reactions, free of anxiety and anticipation, free of pettiness and righteousness, free of anger, free of what you are not and filled for a change with what you were meant to be and in truth already are.

CHAPTER VI

How to Resolve Issues Unmemorably

Unfinished Arguments Accumulate

It's not that issues don't get resolved. Indeed they are settled but settled like ketchup settles into a carpet. An uncleaned carpet can triple in weight within five years, and most relationships get so laden with undigested arguments that they collapse into a dull, angry stupor and cease to move toward their original goal.

"Albert, you've just got to install the cat window. I woke up again at 3 A.M. with Runnymede standing on my chest staring at me. I'm not getting enough alpha sleep."

"Sorry about that, Paula. I'll get to it this weekend."

"But Albert, you've been saying that for a month."

"Well, you know, honey, we could just put the cat out at night like everyone else."

"Oh, sure, and then what if he needed to get in? What if something was after him? What then?"

"What difference will the cat window make? He can still stay out all night if he wants to."

"Yes, Albert, but he can *also* get in if he *needs* to. You know, if you're not going to be a responsible pet owner, you shouldn't have a pet."

"Now there's a thought."

"I see. And I guess you don't mind breaking Gigi's heart."

"That's another thing, Paula, her name is Virginia, not Gigi. Why do we have to have a cat named Runnymede and a daughter named Gigi? Besides, I'll buy her a nice stuffed Garfield after the cat is comfortably settled in at the animal shelter."

"You know, Albert, this conversation is opening my eyes to something I've felt for a very long time."

"What's that, Paula?"

"You only care about mixed soccer. Since joining that team with the silly name you haven't been playing horsey with Gigi and you haven't been scratching Runnymede under the chin where he can't lick. You certainly pretended to like Runnymede well enough when we were dating."

"You were the one who insisted I join the team. You were the one who said it would be good for me to 'get out of the house for a change.' I like the cat. I love my daughter. But I don't want to spend my Saturdays ruining a window with a perfectly good view."

"I guess you don't really care about me either, Albert. And you can stand there calmly peeling your Snickers while wanting Runnymede to be gassed. If I didn't know how much emotion you devote to *mixed* soccer I would say you have become psychotically insensitive and unfeeling. Perhaps you should seek help."

Here Albert, proving that he is neither insensitive nor unfeeling, flings his Snickers at the window in question, grabs his soccer gear, and storms from the house, where in an afternoon match playing goalie for the Yuma Yuccas he fractures the middle three phalanges in his right hand, thus ending the question of installing anything.

Each New Issue Resurrects the Old

We wish we could say that this dialogue was a transcript but it is a composite. If we reprinted verbatim some of the typical arguments we have heard during counseling, they would be dismissed as overwrought fiction. The large number of digressions seen here is actually commonplace and illustrates the typical residue of unsettled questions found in most long-term relationships. The difference between this and the average disagreement is that some of these words might have been thought but left unspoken. Yet the feeling of estrangement by the end of the argument would have been the same.

On this Saturday morning Paula is upset because her sleep continues to be interrupted by the cat asking to be put out. That is the sum of the issue. If the couple had sat down together instead of using the problem as a means of separating still further, they could easily have solved this one difficulty in any of a hundred different mutually acceptable ways. But a hive of older discord lies just beneath their awareness, and therefore settling just one problem in peace is harder than it would seem.

The cry of unresolved issues is strong and persistent. Any couple will feel their failure to have joined. They yearn to bridge the old gaps and fear the potential of further separation more than they welcome the opportunity to reverse the process. To bring up former differences during a discussion is not blameworthy, it is in fact a call for help, but it is mistimed.

Without realizing it—because most arguments are conducted with no deep awareness—Albert and Paula allude to seventeen other issues, none of which had to be brought up to solve *this* problem. In the order they appear, here are the questions they have left unanswered in the past, a small fraction of the total residue if you consider all the others that will be mentioned in future arguments: (1) Why has Albert's promise gone unfulfilled for a month? (2) Should the cat be left out overnight? (3) Is Albert irresponsible? (4) Should the family continue having this pet? (5) Is Albert insensitive to his daughter? (6) Should Paula continue calling Virginia "Gigi"? (7) Should the cat be renamed? (8) Would a stuffed animal sufficiently compensate? (9) Is mixed soccer affecting Albert's attitude toward his daughter and pet? (10) Does the team have a silly name? (11) Is Albert being sufficiently attentive to Paula or has he changed in some fundamental way? (12) Does Paula want Albert around the house? (13) How important is the window view to Albert's happiness? (14) Does Albert still love Paula? (15) Should Albert eat Snickers? (16) Is Albert's contact with other women on Saturdays the root cause of his, in Paula's view, wavering commitment to his family? (17) Does Albert have serious psychological problems?

As can be seen here, it is not easy for most couples to concentrate on a single issue. Nevertheless it is certainly possible and, in itself, to practice doing so will begin giving them a new kind of evidence: that within this relationship there are still grounds for unity and happiness. If one of the partners deviates from this guideline, the other should not make still another issue of this or get caught up in the irrelevant point raised, but should see instead the real desire behind the digression and treat it gently and answer it with love.

Discussions Create the Relationship's Terrain

We have stressed in other chapters the importance of releasing the relationship of its accumulated ill will. If, however, a new wake of resentments and failings continues to be laid, very soon the couple will find themselves in identical straits. Hence the need to have some means of arguing in peace and leaving behind an encouraging history of real friendship.

To resolve issues in the usual way is as damaging to a relationship as not resolving them at all, because the gap is not truly bridged and the unsuccessful attempt merely adds more weight to the couple's doubts about each other. In the argument over the cat window, Paula's concern about the health of her marriage surfaces, a question of far greater importance to her than how she will manage to get more sleep, and yet without fully realizing it she exacerbates this larger problem and works against her own interests. By arguing in the manner they did, this couple, as do most, merely manufactured new issues between them. Albert probably did not mean to take that hard a stand on getting rid of the cat—he may actually have wanted to keep it. And Paula did not have real doubts about Albert's mental health.

The past that drives so many relationships into the ground is built piece by piece, smallness fitted to smallness, selfishness answered with selfishness. Yet the process is largely unconscious. Each couple quickly settles into a few sad methods of conducting arguments, but seldom is the means they use thought through or the results closely examined. One person nags, the other relents. One person reasons, the other becomes silent. One person flares, the other backs down. One person cajoles, the other gives in. But where are the joy and grandeur, where is the friendship that was supposed to flourish, the companionship that through the years was to fuse an invulnerable bond, a solace and a blessing at the close of life? Instead there is a bitter and widening wedge between the two, and even the briefest of discussions contains a hundred dark echoes from the past.

No matter how entrenched are our patterns of problem solving they can be stepped away from easily once we see that they do not serve our interests. The only interest served in most discussions is to be right. But, truly, how deep is this? Do we actually want to make our partner wrong, to defeat a friend, and slowly to defeat a friendship? It certainly may feel that way. Caught up once again in the emotions of a disagreement, we stride doggedly toward our usual means of concluding every argument: adamant silence, crushing logic, patronizing practicality, collapsed crying, quelling anger, martyred acquiescence, loveless humor, sulking retreat.

These postures and a thousand more are attempts to prove a point other than love, and as with all endeavors to show up one's partner, the friendship itself is the victim, because the friendship becomes a mere tool, a means of making the other person feel guilty. The love our partner has for us is now seen as leverage, and in our quiet or noisy way we set about making the relationship a shambles, not realizing that we ourselves are part of the wreckage.

The Magic Rules for Ruining Any Discussion

When we begin experiencing real peace in the presence of our friend we finally start to recognize how devastating is even the smallest friction when it is allowed to continue. At first we think this grain of sand will do nothing, and since this time our partner is clearly the responsible party, we will continue to love and be happy, but not forgive, and shortly all will be well again. Yet inexplicably the peace stays away for hours and the hours lengthen to days. How is this possible when the feeling of separation was so very slight and was over something so very small? A careless word spoken but not taken back (I was misunderstood. I am not obligated to do anything about this). A moment of not listening left unhealed (My distraction was justified. I should not have to explain the obvious to my own wife). A feeling of guilt over an offense now regretted (He violated our understanding. To shorten my husband's remorse would rob him of the lesson). Yet no area of chafing is truly minor. No disagreement is so small that it can be exempted from a loving approach. The presence or absence of love will determine whether an argument is successful or unsuccessful, that is, whether its aftermath will add to or take strength away from the friendship.

The dialogue with which we began this chapter incorporates a few of but not all the rules for disastrous communication— yet only one or two are needed to neutralize the best of intentions. Follow these guidelines, even a little sloppily, and you are guaranteed a miserable time.

1. *Bring the matter up when at least one of you is angry.*
   Variations: Bring it up when nothing can be done about it (in the middle of the night; right before guests are due; when one of you is in the shower).
   Bring it up when concentration is impossible (while driving to a meeting with the IRS; while watching the one TV program you both agree on; while your spouse is balancing the checkbook).

2. *Be as personal as possible when setting forth the problem.*
   Variations: Know the answer before you ask the question.
   While describing the issue, use an accusatory tone.
   Begin by implying who, as usual, is to blame.

3. *Concentrate on getting what you want.*
   Variations: Overwhelm your partner's position before he or she can muster a defense (be very emotional; call in past favors; be impeccably reasonable).
   Impress on your partner what you need and what he or she must do without.
   If you begin losing ground, jockey for position.

4. *Instead of listening, think only of what you will say next.*
   Variations: Do other things while your partner is talking. Forget where your partner left off.
   In other words, listen with all the interest you would give a bathroom exhaust fan.

5. *Correct anything your partner says about you.*
   Variations: Each time your partner gives an example of your behavior, cite a worse example of his or hers.
   Repeat "That's not what I said" often.
   Do not accept anything your partner says at face value

(point out exceptions; point out inaccuracies in facts and in grammar).

6. *Mention anything from the past that has a chance of making your partner defensive.*
   Variations: Make allusions to your partner's sexual performance.
   Remind your husband of his mother's faults.
   Compare what your wife does to what other women do, and after she complains, say, "I didn't mean it that way."

7. *End by saying something that will never be forgotten.*
   Variations: Do something that proves you are a madman.
   Let your parting display proclaim that no exposure of your partner could be amply revealing, no characterization too profane, no consequence sufficiently wretched.
   At least leave the impression you are a little put out.

To Agree Is Not the Purpose

All couples believe they know how to hold a discussion, and yet it is not an exaggeration to say that in most long-term relationships there has rarely been one wholly successful argument. Obviously they are filled with disagreements that end in agreements, but when these are examined, it can be seen that at least a small patch of reservation had to be overlooked in order for accord to be reached.

We believe this is simply how differences are settled, and so even though we sense that our partner is still in conflict, we barge ahead with our newly won concession, thinking the bad moment will pass. Later it becomes painfully clear that it has not and we judge our partner irresolute. Or if we are the one who complied we count our little sacrifice dear and wait for reparation—which never comes or is never quite adequate, and we cannot understand why our partner feels such little gratitude.

The aim of most arguments is to reach outward agreement. Until that is replaced with a desire for friendship, varying degrees of alienation will be the only lasting outcome. Couples quickly develop a sense of helplessness over the pattern that their discussions have fallen into. They believe they are sincerely attempting to break out of it and are simply failing. They try different responses, going from shouting to silence, from interminable talking to walking out of the room, from considering each point raised to sticking tenaciously to one point, but nothing they do seems to alter the usual unhappy ending.

There is no behavioral formula to reversing the habitual course of an argument. It requires a shift in attitude, not in actions, even though actions will modify in the process. No more is needed than one partner's absolute clarity about the purpose of the argument. This is not easy but it is simple. Therefore let us look again at what the aim should be.

Certainly it would make no sense to have a purpose for an argument that is opposed to the purpose of the relationship, and yet for each to try to be right or to get his or her way is not a relationship, it is a separation, and there is a limit to how many of these can be sustained before friendship is turned into a mere alliance between enemies. In a real relationship, broad areas of communication are not kept outside the desires of the heart, and the percentage of any couple's life taken up in mutually affecting decision making is not only broad but pervasive. It cannot remain an exception if there is to be any hope of dependable ease and comfort.

The only allowable purpose for a discussion is to bring you and your partner closer. Minds must come together to decide instead of backing away in order to apply pressure. How is this possible, given the fact that you and your partner are deeply selfish? Fortunately, the selfishness is compartmentalized and your hearts remain unaffected. You need not eliminate it;

merely bypass it because you recognize that it is not in your interests to be selfish. To the ego, this concept is insane because it sees no value in love. But love is in your interests because you *are* love, or at least part of you is, and thus each discussion is a way of moving into your real self.

Do you want what the discussion is ostensibly *about?* Do you want to take its subject as your aim? Or do you want to be more yourself and know your partner's self? You cannot have both, for one is love and the other is attack in however reasonable a disguise.

A little time is obviously needed to see one's true interests. If you rush into a discussion you will operate from your insensitivity by habit and aim for a prize your heart cares nothing about. Do not kid yourself. You *do* know whether the discussion is ending with the two of you feeling closer. The selfish part of your mind will tell you that the little sadness and sense of distance you may now feel was a small price to pay for the concession you won or the point you made. Or it will argue that it was all unavoidable. This may happen many times before you begin reversing your ordinary way of participating. This transition is an important stage of growth and entails looking more and more carefully at selfish impulses and their aftermath. Is how you feel really worth it? Was the way it went truly unavoidable?

Thus you will come to see the result you want, and this deeper recognition will begin to eclipse your pettiness in the midst of an argument. Gradually you will catch the mistakes sooner, and eventually you will learn to avoid them from the start. For you *do* want these times of deciding to warm your hearts and lighten your steps. So persist in the guidelines we will give, and these little defeats to your relationship will slowly give way to friendship.

We are so used to thinking of a discussion as a symbol of separation that it can often be helpful to change its form enough that something new will appear to be happening and thus the old mind set is undercut. To take the usual process, break it into steps and put them in order is usually all that is needed to accomplish this.

An issue could be said to pass through five stages in reaching resolution. First, it must be thought of by at least one of the partners as an issue. Second, a moment is chosen to bring the matter up. Third, a decision is made as to the manner in which it will be presented. Fourth, there is an exchange of thoughts and feelings. And fifth, the discussion is concluded.

Most couples give very little thought to the first three stages. They simply find themselves in the thick of a so-called spontaneous argument and no one is certain at what point it began. Obviously you must become more conscious of the subjects you bring up so carelessly. Any sign of fear over what you are about to say is a very useful indicator. If you see you have a question about whether to say it, let this be your cue to break these preliminary choices into conscious steps. Do not begrudge the time; remember instead how strongly you want to begin building a real friendship.

Five Steps in Preparing to Argue

First, you might ask yourself if the issue you are thinking of is actually a present issue or merely one you have been reminded of. In other words, be certain this is currently a problem and not one the relationship may already be on its way to solving. Many people habitually rake over their marriage for signs of imperfection and naturally they find a great many, but it can be far more disrupting to friendship to be constantly questioning and comparing than to wait to see if the problem continues in any severe way. Meanwhile, enjoy what is already between you without telling yourself what this is.

Never describe your relationship to yourself or to others. Never assign to it a specific identity. Do not think you know. Instead of believing that you must decide whether it is good or bad, treat it gently, as if you did *not* know it, as if conceivably its value was more precious than you could see.

If the issue is unquestionably a present one, the second step you might try is to let go of it. Letting go is not "better," but it is an option that current values tend to underrate. However, it must be accomplished thoroughly and honestly or the issue will grow like mold in a dark unseen place. If it is done consciously dismissal is not denial. Essentially it entails examining in detail what you do not like and then making a deliberate effort to identify with another part of you that never "takes issue" with any living thing, that is still and at ease, that acts only from peace.

Nothing is an issue for everyone. We can be sure that thousands would not see it the way we think it *must* be seen. If a couple espouses world energy consciousness or is on a tight budget, for one of the partners to habitually leave the hot water running, not turn off lights, or keep the refrigerator door open may be grating or even shocking to the other partner. Yet the spectacle of someone wasting energy and money is *not* grating or shocking. The interpretation we assign it, and not the act itself, determines the emotions we feel. Jordan, age two, is "shockingly irresponsible." He has even been known (yesterday, in fact) to flush a toilet five times in a row and then run to tell his big brother about the accomplishment. "John, I flush, I flush!" "That's nice," said John, blatantly contributing to the delinquency of a minor. The reason Jordan didn't tell his father (who is the family's conscience in these matters) was that he was the very one who kept showing him how it was done, thereby encouraging him to waste over fifteen gallons of water (plus six more his father used researching that figure). Even Tuba the Siamese, who sniffs anything she doesn't understand, came in once to perform her ritual and walked away without so much as a yowl of protest.

So here we have four reactions issuing from four interpretations: pride from the father, support from the seven-year-old, excitement from the two-year-old and, having no originality, curiosity from the cat. Clearly no uniform effect was produced by an external and unreachable cause. How then might you let go of your reaction to your spouse's wasteful habits in lieu of bringing it up one more time? Certainly you would not try dishonestly to convince yourself that the practice was not costing money or energy. Or that it did not really matter to you. Neither would you attempt to assign some motive to your partner's acts that you did not believe, such as not knowing any better or really trying hard but being unable to stop. Dishonesty does not end an unhappy line of thought. That is why reinterpretation is generally not effective.

You will need new and more important grounds from which to respond so that your reaction will be genuine, for it must be kept in mind that not to bring something up—while continuing to harbor resentment—is a dynamic that ruins many of this world's relationships. Therefore you might take a moment to remember your goal. Is it to use the relationship as a means of balancing your budget? Or as a way of retarding world resource depletion? Is it to use it at all? Or is love the goal, and do you now wish to take time off from love to be right?

If in your moment of consideration you are able to see these facts deeply enough, you may open your eyes to your partner's innocence and no longer feel compelled to *understand* why he or she does these things. But if after making the attempt to free your mind you see that you have not let the issue go, then perhaps to bring it up would be the preferable course, for undoubtedly that is better than storing anger or fear.

Of course if your spouse is someone who cannot be approached in this way, then you will need to consider other means of relinquishing it, and the next to the last section in this chapter includes suggestions on how to handle anger and grievances wholly on your own.

The third step is to consider if this is the time. If you feel an urge to bring it up quickly, be very alert to anger. Your heart is willing to wait but your ego is not, especially if it senses an opportunity to strike back. The ego is merely our love of misery, of withdrawal and loneliness, and it can feel like our own deep impulse even though it exists on the most superficial level of the mind.

For too long now our relationships have been jerked around by our own lack of awareness. There is more to your mind than selfishness. So be still a moment and let peace arise from you. Is this the time? A simple question. There need not be great soul-searching and hand-wringing over it. If your partner has just done something and this is the issue, clearly he or she is likely to be more defensive if instantly called on it. If your partner is not in a particularly happy frame of mind, is hostile, worried or depressed, a more receptive state will surely come and nothing is lost by waiting. Is this the time? Merely look and know the answer. The urge to attack when you are angry is very strong, but if you will allow yourself time to reflect on your genuine feelings, this will do more to relieve your frustration.

The fourth step is to be certain that communication is your aim. Trying to get someone to change is not communication because you have already decided what change is needed. Your partner is therefore left with nothing to say and will definitely feel your unwillingness to consider, to listen, to appreciate. So before you speak take time to hear your heart.

You are not two advocates arguing a case. You are interested in joining, not in prevailing. You are like the directors of a business you both love coming together to help it over a difficult situation. You don't care from whose lips the solution comes. You welcome the *answer*. To this end what are you willing to do if your partner becomes defensive? Are you prepared, and have you prepared, to carry through your love of the relationship?

How many traffic snarls have you been willing to wait out or thread your way through to reach home? Yet that was a building, not a real home. Now be willing to reach home. If analyzing the kind of friend you will be during the discussion could help, then see each possibility in advance and picture responding in peace. Be careful not to adopt an attitude of superiority or righteousness. If your goal is oneness, what does it matter that on this occasion you were the one who tried? Say then, "I will not use my efforts to love as a reason to attack." Be prepared also to forgive yourself and to start over quickly if you forget. Guilt is a form of withdrawal that will not take you home.

The final point to consider is whether you are clear that the problem is the relationship's and not your partner's. In our example the problem was not Paula's, because her lack of sleep was affecting Albert also. One person's jealousy, appetite, hypersensitivity, frigidity, phobia or any other characteristic that has become an issue cannot successfully be viewed as more one's responsibility than the other's because friendship is always a mutual sharing of all burdens.

Very often what one person acts out merely reflects a deeper disturbance within both partners. But seldom is this obvious. The couple's attention is usually focused on the symptom and thus they miss seeing that no one acts in isolation. Yet whatever two minds produce, two minds can heal. Naturally this should not be interpreted to mean that one partner must never go alone to a doctor, a therapy group, or other source of help. But all steps should be given both partners' support, and if a change is tried the reason for the change need not be thought of as one partner's responsibility more than another's.

You must understand that unless you make a specific effort to see through the fallacy, you *will* go into a discussion thinking one of you is more to blame than the other, and this will make it very hard to listen and be open. Learn to treat every issue as an impersonal and neutral enemy and to close ranks against it. An addiction, for example, can be viewed as you would a hurricane or a deluge—you need each other's help to survive the storm. Our dog, Sunny Sunshine Pumpkin Prather (whose very name is a masterpiece of family compromise), gets sprayed by a skunk about once a month and the smell is everyone's problem. What good would it do to blame the dog? And yet we have seen other families get angry at their dog "for being so stupid."

Is a person less worthy of devotion than a dog? When has judging anyone ever helped? So resolve to be a friend, to say in your heart, "Your love is my love, and your pain is my pain, and together we will wipe the tears away."

These preliminary steps, which should only take an instant or two to complete, will at least make it possible for a discussion to begin with some chance of success. Now you are ready for a *real* argument, one in which your minds can join rather than separate.

The Six Rules of Arguing

1. HAVE PEACE AND CONCENTRATION

Before you begin eliminate as many distractions as possible. Sit down if you can, unplug the phone, and perhaps close your eyes for a moment and bring your minds to rest. You simply want to be certain that your attention is on what you are doing —that you are not setting up for guests, eating breakfast, driving a car, getting ready for bed, doing housework or caring for your children at the same time you are attempting to resolve a difference between you.

What your body does symbolizes to your partner and to you where your priorities lie at the moment. Therefore demonstrate in these little ways that you take seriously the business before you.

2. STATE YOUR EGO POSITION

Both of you must take a stand before there can be a disagreement. If even one of you forgot to cherish your position, no sense of separation would occur. But since there *is* a disagreement, you now wish to lay it out where it is accessible to your joint sanity.

In an unsuccessful argument the ego positions are never stated honestly. Whenever you justify or attack you are being insincere because you are not stating what you are afraid of. In fact, you are pretending to be unafraid. But if you were you would not be fighting to keep your opinion.

Thus the first step is to describe the stand you have taken without trying to sound right. Be open and honest, but as much as is possible avoid building a case and implying that what you say is well founded, just, proper, reasonable or fair. Simply give your position without embellishment.

You do not want to make a fetish of this but if you can state it in terms of what you are afraid of rather than what you demand, this will make joining easier. We are willing to relinquish fear—once it is seen as fear—but we think we are sacrificing if we compromise on what we want. So, for example, instead of saying, "The way you eat is disgusting," you could try to look more deeply at what goes on in you when your partner eats in this manner. After doing so, you see that you are, let us say, afraid that this is a sign of disrespect. And so you might say, "When you eat with your mouth open, I am afraid that I mean very little to you." Or you see that you are embarrassed about what others will think, and so this is the fear you state.

You do not wish to attack your partner even indirectly while giving your ego opinions. And be careful not to confuse yourself that opinions can come from any other source except ego. Any stand that separates does not come from love, so do not withhold expressing a feeling if, as you begin talking, you suddenly see its superficiality. State it even though it seems embarrassing. You are not in an appearance contest. You are trying to bridge a gap, and absolute honesty is required. In this context a feeling of embarrassment over what you are about to say may indicate that this time you have been willing to go a little deeper.

Remember, too, that to look at your fears and state them plainly does not call for long and irrelevant confessions.

Dredging up your sins is a form of attack that is as harmful to your relationship as one directed at your partner's mistakes. The rule is to stay with the subject at hand. Remorse is not a virtue and if wallowed in can quickly become a barrier to joining. Judging is the problem, not the answer, so avoid it in any guise no matter who or what the target.

The final guideline is to take your time, but do *not* bring in other issues and grievances that seem to be connected to the one at hand. These *will* come to mind and they will usually be accompanied by the thought that perhaps it would be more honest to state them. This is where your five steps of preparation will come to your aid, for if you can remember that your sole purpose is to help the relationship by fostering a feeling of connectedness and friendship, you will have no difficulty foreseeing the disrupting effect of jogging your partner's mind with other memories and symbols of anger. To resolve one issue is enough. Let there be success here, and then the next step can be taken in its time.

3. LISTEN

Allow your partner to be at ease while he or she is talking. Do not wait tensely for your turn, because this will be felt and is not the practicing of friendship. Certainly do not interrupt, for don't you already know what *you* have to say? What you do not know is what your partner is saying. You may think you have heard it all before but if you had heard *any* of it before, this discussion would be unnecessary.

On an ego level when two marry it is a marriage of convenience. They wish the union because they believe it is to their personal advantage, and they do not truly want to join because to do so would make another's interests as great as their own. They are like two nations trying to maintain détente. Whenever one nation believes it is *now* in its interests to break with the appearance of mutual caring, it will do so. And this is what has occurred when two people become hostile; they have each made something more important than how their partner feels.

Watch your thoughts carefully for any inclination to dismiss what is being said or to center on the unimportant details, the mere form, and to miss the content. Most couples do not believe what their partners say. They think it is insincere, a front for another motive. It is Gayle's and my experience that during an argument most people do mean what they say, and even when they lie what they are trying so hard to communicate is quite evident if only the other would look.

We therefore advise the partner whose turn it is to listen to repeat silently to himself or herself, "[Name] really means what [he or she] is saying."

Finally, do not keep track of how your partner deviates from these guidelines or any other rules you may have agreed on. The purpose of rules is to promote peace, and manufacturing additional issues from them is a sad misuse. The typical state of mind that passes for listening is rehearsing. Rehearsing the other's spoken errors, rehearsing the misrepresentations of oneself, rehearsing the points that one will answer and the points that one will make, rehearsing the wounds and how they will be revenged. Many honestly believe they are listening when in fact they are merely thinking defensively, watching the other for signs of aggression and positioning themselves for another attack. Listening is not related to the future in any way. It is fascinated with the present and preoccupied with peace.

The ego side of us believes that love and care can be separated, that it is possible to love and yet be casual and neglectful. Unless we care for and are care-full, whatever emotion we are experiencing, it is certainly not love. Listening is a way of attending and ministering to another. It is more than a sentiment; it is a gift. So listen with the heart, not the intellect or the memory. Hear what is said, believe it, and appreciate it deeply.

4. REMEMBER LOVE

In an argument that burdens the relationship rather than lightens it, each partner takes a stand and in effect says, "You must come to my side, you must bow to me," and any concession made feels like giving in. A loss of power and perhaps even dignity is experienced, and the next time around one is determined not to lose still more of "oneself." In most long-term relationships not-to-give-in becomes the underlying purpose of all arguments.

A successful argument avoids the issue of loss altogether. It is an exercise in gaining love, gaining friendship, and like a good workout, it leaves a sense of satisfaction and invigoration. But love is hard to remember during an argument because the differences in egos are the center of attention, and as a consequence, the alikeness of the hearts fades from view. It is therefore essential that love be remembered despite the difficulty, and to do so deliberately is the most critical component of any planned argument.

After you have each stated your ego positions, close your eyes and make an all-out attempt to recall the value of this friendship. You want now to take your attention off your partner's weaknesses—selfishness, obstinacy, anger, whatever it may be—and turn your gaze to what you once saw, and is still there to see, of this person's gentleness and goodness.

An effective exercise is to list to yourself examples of your partner's strengths, the qualities you love most about this person. Begin with the most current and go back in time. Was he or she recently thoughtful to some person or animal? Can you recall an instant of happiness, of light? These do not have to be dramatic demonstrations of saintliness, just simple evidences of honesty or generosity or kindness, anything at all that allows you to see why it is no accident that you are here.[1]

[1] I have often used this exercise apart from arguing as a general way of increasing my sense of oneness with Gayle (or with our children). For in-

To remember that you love someone with whom you are angry can require a great effort. Therefore exert yourself and truly concentrate until you can feel your mind loosening its grip on judgment and misery. It may seem to be trickery to jog the mind in this way, and it is. But there is nothing wrong with tricks, devices and techniques. Chaos feels quite normal to the ego, and a moment's discipline can seem strange. To do something with your mind that you do not ordinarily do is not a form of dishonesty. In this case it leads to truth.

There is no greater or more powerful truth than the simple fact that you are not alone. And that is all you are trying to recall. So do what allows this gentle memory to return. If blinds must be raised, raise them; if curtains must be pulled back, pull them back; if walls must be pushed down, push them down. You harm nothing, you only become incapable of harm, when you take control of your undisciplined mind. So if picturing a holy figure of light standing behind and walking into your partner will allow you to see what is already there, then do this easily. If imagining what your partner was like as a little child, or recalling the period when the two of you first met, will help, then help. Say the words, use the images, make the effort to bring a little truth before your mental eyes so weary of hate, and be comfortable with innocence, which washes away an enemy and shows you the face of a friend.

5. PREPARE YOUR GIFTS AND GIVE THEM

Continue for a moment longer with your eyes closed, for you now wish to consider once again the issue that is between you and your partner. What can you do to dissolve this one barrier? What are you willing to do? If the issue is financial, are you willing to modify your spending habits and in what ways

---

stance, I may set my watch to go off every half hour, at which time I stop what I am doing and recall ten examples of the things I love about her. That comes to one hundred examples every five hours and, as you might expect, has a cumulative effect on our relationship as well as being a very pleasant task.

specifically would you do that? Are you willing to look for a higher-paying job, and just what steps will that entail and exactly when will you take the first one? Is the issue that one of your parents keeps speaking against your spouse? Then how will you bring this to an end; what will you say or do and when will you say or do it?

If you took the time to remember the importance of this relationship, these kinds of considerations now will be like shopping for presents to give to your beloved. No longer is it possible to misinterpret these very precise gestures you will make as compromises and defeats. They are gifts to the relationship, bricks of strength you will contribute to the foundation of your friendship. Select them carefully and be certain they fill out the needed gaps. Do not be vague or idealistic in your offerings. Be quite concrete because the issue is concrete.

Gayle and I were present when one husband opened his eyes and said that he would strive to be a good and loyal father and in the years to come would bring to their child every possible advantage to develop its talents. Yet all his wife was complaining about was having to care for the baby entirely by herself. After closing his eyes and trying again, he volunteered to get up with the baby on the weekends and to change its diapers in the evenings when he was home from work. This was so touching to his wife that she cried, whereas his previous gift, although it was sincere, had left her unmoved.

Or the wife who said that hereafter she would be more supportive of her husband's fears, when what he was upset about was the number of accidents and near-misses she was having while driving. When asked by us to make her gifts more specific, she paused a moment and then said she would start wearing her glasses and using her seat belt. The husband, who before could not think of a single gift, suddenly had the insight that his wife did not like the car she was driving and offered to switch.

These particular gestures are not what eliminated the issues in the two cases. Many others would have worked as well. The determining lesson both couples had to learn was to look more closely at what their spouse was saying and to try to help in a way that would be truly meaningful, not to them but to their spouse.

Issues can be resolved in many ways besides "meeting each other halfway." Often one of the partners will see that he or she simply does not feel very strongly about it and the fact that the other does is sufficient reason to go along. It is not uncommon for an issue to suddenly seem meaningless to both and for them to see that, really, there is nothing to decide. Sometimes new alternatives are seen that neutralize the old question. It might occur to Paula and Albert to hire someone to put in the cat window and they would count the money well spent. The couple with the baby might remember a relative's repeated offer to help.

The major block to being open to new alternatives is the desire to continue being right. Solution literally is not wanted because as long as the issue stays alive, each partner can be virtuous, logical, martyred, vindictive or whatever other form being right takes. See through this insanity quickly and know how much better you like the feeling of closeness.

You wish a resolution that symbolizes love and concern. You wish a peaceful rather than a clever ending, although very creative solutions should be considered. And you also do not want to undo what you have accomplished by matching it against some imagined ideal, for we have seen many couples who had to make multiple attempts over a period of months before a point of contention was smoothed away, and in some cases the boost to their marriage was immense even though they had not had a dramatic one-shot resolution. Each effort they made contributed a little because it provided evidence that the other appreciated the relationship enough to try.

6. PROTECT YOUR GAINS

There should be no sense of rush or competition during the period in which both partners have their eyes closed. Two decisions must be made—to remember love and to select the gifts each will give to the relationship—and because this entails what one is to receive as well as to give there can be an unconscious assessment of the amount of time each partner takes, the ego assumption being that the one who takes longest loves least, which is utter nonsense. So let the entire argument begin, run its course and end, in peace and ease. And when it is over, protect your gains by not gnawing on every word spoken, every decision made. You did your best, as did your partner, and now honor the peace and love you attempted and fail to dive back into loveless reassessment and second-guessing.

If you can, refrain from asking yourself whether the gifts are equal, whether you came out better or worse than your partner, and at least try to make good what you gave in love. Then if it turns out to be too great a burden, go to your friend and together decide what would help the relationship most.

If your partner does not think that he or she can live with the gifts as offered and now wishes to take back some, do not let this shock you. Continue being a friend. Sometimes we expect too much of ourselves and must make adjustments, so rather than condemn, rush to lighten the load.

To force another or oneself to carry out a task in conflict will benefit no one. Either the task must be modified or the conflict relinquished. Next time perhaps you can look more closely at your gifts before you offer them to see if you believe they are within the bounds of your willingness to carry out. Remember that selfishness is not the only pleasure. There is also pleasure in doing something for another even though it is difficult.

Resolving Issues Within Yourself

It is easier to free your mind of an issue or grievance if your partner is willing to admit his or her participation and help in the relinquishing process. However, when this is not a possibility it is still wholly within your ability to do this work on your own, and it is essential to your happiness and to the growth of your relationship that you do so.

The steps needed are basically the same as those we have been discussing. First, you wish to look carefully at the argument that is taking place in your mind. Saying it out loud or writing it out will often help you see it more clearly. As part of this process, it is beneficial to sit down and imagine each of the various outcomes that would be acceptable to you. After you have identified several, note that they conflict and that no real certainty exists. You are certain that you are upset but if you are able to be honest in considering what you want to come of the upset, you will see that your ego has no real clarity or consistency.

Second, release the anger in some formal and thorough way. It is fine to do this dramatically in such ways as hitting or clubbing a pillow or mattress, imagining your partner as you chop wood, and coupling any of these with yelling or other sounds that help free the mind. It is also fine to dance it out, run it out, cry it out, walk it out—anything that gives a sense of release and relinquishment and does not enlarge the problem by embroiling other people. To talk it out with a friend who will not take sides and who will keep your confidence is another option, but if there is any question as to this person's effect on you, perhaps you should try the simpler means first.

Often a gentle imagery in which one's partner is repeatedly surrounded in light, light is pictured while the partner's name is repeated, or light is seen in place of the partner can be equally as beneficial as something more physical. A little experimentation is good as long as some magical or perfect technique is not being sought. As in all things, there is no one right way to proceed.

Third, recall the value of the relationship and your debt of gratitude to your partner. Remember at least its potential to hurt you if you do not do this work. Use any trick that will help you reach your core of sincerity, such as making two fists and opening one finger with each incident of thoughtfulness or caring, humor or gentleness, goodness or restraint that you recall your partner ever having displayed.

Once you have done the best you can, honor the effort by gently refusing to sink back into the grudge or question you have released. Anger can be quite thoroughly released and still your ego might test your sincerity for a time. When you have seen that a line of thought is of no use to you, do not lightly throw away this insight. It is your right to be intelligent.

Study, Humility, and Concentration

Expect very little from your first few planned arguments. You do not have in your hands a magic wand. But each effort will help somewhat, and even one success can help immeasurably. The couple that goes forward toward real friendship learns to take the little gains and ceases waiting in misery for a single transforming experience that will prove their relationship special. Ordinary love is quite nice.

It is important to be willing to devote all the time needed to learning this new way of arguing, because it can provide your relationship with the fertile ground upon which it can begin to grow and flower. Your choice is simple. It is to spend your lives together accumulating grievances, or to make of your differences a proving ground for your commitment and oneness.

Expectations can ruin almost anything, and marriage in particular is a showcase for this dynamic. Many jobs and most careers require years of study and application before advancement can be anticipated. We fret very little over this because we do not expect it to be otherwise. A marriage, on the other hand, is looked at like a vacation. We have *only* expectations and believe nothing is required of us. In almost no other area of life is such an absurd assumption made. Even when we go to a supermarket we know in advance that every item on the list will have to be tracked down. Lip service is unquestionably paid to the concept that marriage must be worked at, but no couple actually believes this applies to them, and if it does, they are having to begin at a point vastly inferior to most other relationships and certainly beneath what they individually deserve.

For most couples, "to work at" means to be willing to endure the misery. It does not mean to study and to repeatedly start over until what has not been learned is finally learned. Marriage is not a candy store where we are waited on and can concern ourselves merely with what we get. And yet isn't this how most people talk about their relationships, citing all they are not getting, never citing all they are not giving? If you believe nothing else in this book please believe this: There is not one real relationship on this earth that came into being without study, humility, and concentration.

CHAPTER VII

Settled Patterns and Unhappy Dynamics

Blind Commitment

"Why do adults get to pick out the tree?" John asked one Christmas. And thus began our family tradition of having three trees. The one John chose was so small that Gayle's and my twenty-year collection of ornaments would have "mashed that sucker flat," and so for ourselves we got the long-term-relationship size. Then John pointed out that the upper branches of his tree were inaccessible to Jordan. We patiently explained that having separate trees was not in the true spirit of Christmas. His exact rebuttal: "I've only been alive for five Christmases and I don't know about these things." When he saw us laughing he knew he had us and sent Jordan back into the tree lot to hunt his own.

That year we managed to salvage the spirit of Christmas by putting the trees as close together as possible, which, as it turned out, meant that differences in decorating techniques became highly noticeable. Except for a brief but firm discussion over how many times it was reasonable for Mommy and

Daddy to have to hear the Disney chipmunks sing "We Wish You a Merry Christmas," we decorated without incident until John got to the icicles. Gayle, obviously shocked, stopped to demonstrate the proper technique, while in the background I lectured on how real icicles are formed. But John said he was *not* "globbing his on," he was making spider webs in the branches and reminded us that he was confining his efforts to *his* branches.

Meanwhile Jordan, who had been hearing "bicycles" instead of "icicles," was on his hands and knees pushing little pieces of them across the rug and making the appropriate sound effects. Yet periodically he would run to the bathroom and hold them under the faucet. Curious, I asked, "Why are you putting water on your bicycles?"

"To get them wet," he said. Then I realized he had heard me explaining that icicles were made from dripping water and that the more water that passed over them the bigger they grew.

At this point John decided to rescue Jordan from his misapprehension and started yelling, "No, Jordy, they're not *bi*cycles, they're *ic*icles." But Jordan saw this for what it was, a ploy by his big brother to get the bicycles for himself, and quickly moved his operation to a remote corner of the living room.

Our children obviously do these things because they know we are writers and are in constant need of interesting analogies. And the foregoing does illustrate quite well the first point we wish to make: To be centered in the past blocks communication.

When Gayle and I were kids, icicles were made of metal (lead, as I recall) and were large enough and expensive enough that most parents insisted that they be put on the tree one at a time. And in this final ceremony there was indeed a certain exquisite pleasure in handling these shining delicate strands, taking only a few at a time out of the package, and making sure that each one was placed on a branch—just so.

Then the jolt of suddenly seeing John dumping great handfuls on the center of the boughs.

Our recital on the proper uses of icicles hurt John's feelings sufficiently (he collapsed to a sitting position and hung his head—just so) that we both realized we were making a mistake. What John was putting on his tree were not the things we were remembering. His were very inexpensive, very lightweight, and almost impossible to separate without breaking. They did indeed look somewhat like a particular kind of spider web that John loved coming across on his hikes. Jordan, on the other hand, *wanted* them to remain bicycles because it is far more fun to push something you know around on the floor than to give something you don't know to a tree. In the days to come he remained adamant that these were bicycles, and of course they were just as much that as they were spikes of ice or spider webs. We each saw what we individually cherished from the past.

In this case we all had positive associations with what we were seeing in place of what was there, and yet these "good" memories were no less disrupting than "bad" ones would have been, because they were equally as preoccupying. The thought "This is not the way my mother cooked hash browns" is the same in its effect as "He's just like my father, he's never quite pleased." Our absorption with any aspect of our past prevents us from seeing accurately what our mate does. It is very important that you accept this idea as a working hypothesis even if you do not yet see the extent to which you are reacting from your past. If you can merely *assume* some degree of distortion in all your perceptions you will not be as quick to judge, as quick to take stands and be right, as quick to turn away and be discouraged, and this will provide a little space in which healing can begin.

Healing is merely a shift in what you think is important. You do love your partner, but clearly you are not consistently sensitive to this fact. Awareness of your own capacity is being blocked by the emphasis you still unconsciously place on other relationships, especially those you had during your formative years. Once your mind sees importance where it actually is, the healing will be complete and home will again be where the heart is.

Unlearning the Roles of Husband and Wife

Few realize the work entailed in freeing one's perceptions, and thus one's reactions, from early lessons received on what a wife is for, what a husband is for, what children are for, what a home is for and so forth. Just as we unconsciously pick up a certain accent along with our syntax and vocabulary, we also pick up precise attitudes toward housework, money matters, evening activities, possessions, and so on. Children do not learn the husband and wife roles in some abstract form. They see how *this* wife and *this* husband are treated, as well as icicles, pets and everything else, and to the little child this is simply the way it is and therefore the way it *should* be.

As a child, I learned how to break up, not how to stay together, because that is essentially what my mother and father were in the process of doing for the eight years I saw them relating to each other. I learned the words and tone of voice one uses to inflict pain and on what occasions one does this. I learned over what issues one becomes silently angry, how one goes about staying away and how to withdraw while still in the house. Most of these and other unhappy lessons I have as little memory of learning as I do of having been taught to say "X-a-ray" instead of "X-ray" or "aig" instead of "egg." My mistakes in language continued for many years after having been informed of them, just as they did with my posture and dietary habits. At age forty-eight I can say that I now have done a reasonable job of unlearning bad diet, bad posture and mispronunciations, but the lessons on how to treat one's spouse and children have been far more complex and difficult and I am only about half finished, even though I have been making them my first priority for several years now.

Most of the readers of this book probably will have a little less to unlearn in these areas than I had, some of course will have more, but no one need feel hopeless. There is unquestionably much effort and starting over required but also there are definite signs of gain along the way. Among other areas of progress, Gayle and I have learned how to be alone together at home, how to be in a car together, how to do housework together, to discipline and care for our children together, to eat out, to have long chatty conversations, and to resolve issues peacefully. There are still three or four areas in which we do not practice happiness well. Shopping together is one of them. Illness is another. (We both tend to become judgmental of the one who is sick.) But the time is not far off when these will be added to our list of freedoms. As little as three years ago, we could not have said that we were happy eating in a restaurant together or driving long distances, because the antecedents of our programmed ways of looking at these activities had not yet been closely observed. Yet now they have and today these are consistently enjoyable times. There is at least one way of proceeding that will take most couples forward and its basic component is their willingness to trace back the roots of every attitude that hinders the growth of peace within the relationship.

The usual resistance to taking this step runs like this: "If the approach is old hat, if it has been widely tried and found of value, I want no part of it. I want a newer approach, one with otherworldly overtones, or at least one backed by an exciting new theory and an impressive nomenclature, and above all, one that assures dramatic results." Thus some readers will think that what we are speaking of here smacks of primeval couches and years of analysis and is therefore an outmoded approach. Analysis, if it is conducted intelligently by one who is sensitive and loving, can do much, and for thousands has clearly done much, to release the mind of its bond with the past. In our opinion two who are beyond the honeymoon stage —if they are determined to build a friendship—can achieve equally effective results. The procedure in either context is much the same: Guilt and blame must be renounced and in their place the effects of past conditioning must be seen as the core of the relationship's problems.

So indeed we are suggesting a gentle form of co-analysis as a very efficient means of progress, and one that we have been using ourselves and teaching others for several years now. However, it is certainly unnecessary for any couple to use these rather ho-hum terms. Let us call it instead Radical Psyche Tracing, or "the newly published and controversial RPT theory by Prather and Prather." When called upon to explain what you are up to, begin with, "Oh! You don't know about that?" And then, showing your total freedom from all relationship problems, reach over and affectionately rub your partner's neck as you give your précis in informed but matter-of-fact tones.

Presuming Mutual Participation

If one of you has been through formal analysis, it is important that you *not* assume a position of leadership or of superior insight. What we are proposing in this chapter is so simple as to require no background knowledge or training of any kind and is best approached as a new device that you will learn and practice together.

There are those who believe they are already free of the past and that what they see in their partner as faults are realities independent of their own distorting judgments. However, in the terms we are speaking of here, no one is beyond the separating influences of his past unless he can say that he never becomes fearful, never feels guilt, never thinks of hurting or punishing any living creature. Until that point has been reached both parties must assume they are participating in sustaining every dynamic that characterizes their relationship.

There is a part of all of us that loves dearly the pastime of handling blame. We love to mull it over, probe its sinful depths, discuss it for long and miserable hours, assume it and shift it and do everything but doubt it. This part of us still believes "Who is most to blame?" to be a meaningful question. Yet it is no more meaningful than saying, "The old car still runs because you gave it a tank of gas and four new tires, whereas all I did is add the battery." The game of fixing fault, of pinning the tail on the donkey, must be seen as unhelpful and the gentler, happier game of "Look at the mess we made, let's clean it up together" put in its place.

Naturally, any upset can be perceived as caused wholly by one and not at all by the other. And in the minds of most couples this will be the interpretation—that somehow, in some way, the other is to blame. Many of the relationship's problems will appear one-sided because of society's long-standing practice of so classifying them, even though the validity of some of these attitudes is presently being questioned, but not, however, the arbitrariness of blame itself. For example, it has long been thought that if a man had an affair, although an indiscretion on his part, it was essentially his wife's fault for not keeping him sexually satisfied. Now the position is shifting to blaming the acting spouse, man or woman. But the third person, if single, is due only mild censure for opportunism. As one song puts it, "If you're gonna do him wrong again, you might as well do him wrong with me." Or another example: if the husband gambled or was alcoholic and failed in his role as family provider, the wife was considered blameless, perhaps even saintly. And this stance, despite AA and other educational groups, has remained basically unmodified.

Society's position is irrelevant to the work you must do. So too is the position taken by friends and relatives. If you look for justification to continue seeing your partner at fault you will find it, and you already have enough to sort through within your own reactions not to add further confusion by asking another to take sides. Few can decline the gift of attack. Therefore offer not the other half of your relationship as a target, for it will be your own devotion and love you forfeit.

Do not underestimate how deeply entrenched is this first reaction to all things done by the spouse. Yet first reactions *can* be allowed to pass and the more genuine second reaction given a hearing. Through much practice one can learn to do this consistently and in fact must learn to if progress is not to remain grindingly slow. Our first reaction, prized by the ego for its lightning speed, always springs from fear and is defensive and hindering in its effects. You will learn to feel your way a little more slowly once you begin experiencing the many gifts your second and deeper response can offer. So allow yourself to assume, at least intellectually, that if some upset is occurring, or if some unspoken mood or distance exists between you and your friend, you have indeed played your part. Its exact nature and precise dimensions are unimportant. Do not get sidetracked into endlessly defining them because this is still another version of determining blame. Look at it as you might an unmade bed, formed by both of you—but while you slept. Who truly knows which of you contributed most, and who would truly care?

The Answer to Every Call for Help Is Gentleness

Participation is always innocent, because the individuals are merely acting out lessons taught them by others. These unhappy patterns can pass from generation to generation for many hundreds of years before someone recognizes that the emotions he is feeling are not his own and declines to participate further. Your partner does many things that elicit no ego response from you, and because you are naturally and peacefully neutral, because you do not participate by cherishing even one thought of judgment or fear, the relationship develops no new unhappy dynamics in these areas. Yet there are other relationships in which the couples are not able to allow these same circumstances to pass and old dynamics are strengthened or new ones formed.

The key that both parties are participating is that both are emotionally involved. If one is upset and the other sees this as a call for help, and *does* help, only greater joining ensues. However, if a partner does something provoking, depressing, irritating, saddening, the other has by definition participated by interpreting it in this way—even though not responding outwardly and perhaps believing as well that he or she did nothing to set up the situation initially. Although participation is sometimes outward, taking place before or after the incident, it is *always* mental, and it is always a choice.

Gayle and I recently gave some workshops in Hawaii where the beaches and their happy effects on Jordan and John answered all questions about what to do during our off hours. Because we live in the Southwest, it had been several years since I had seen young, attractive women in bikinis and I was surprised at my fascination. I began feeling guilty about my desire to look at them and tried to hide any attempts to do so from Gayle. Gayle, on the other hand, did not participate in this potential problem. She seemed to be happy for me whether I was diving and ogling the fish, taking walks with John and ogling the wild flowers, or sitting on the beach and feeling guilty and miserable ogling the bodies.

There was, of course, another part of my mind that could see the craziness of all this, that it is impossible *not* to notice what the world screams is noteworthy, that it is the *way* one notices that helps or hinders, and that to view *anything* anxiously jeopardizes peace. I worked along these lines for several days, but my progress was so slow that I decided to ask Gayle for help, because I knew that even though what I looked at might not concern her, my feelings of self-blame would eventually pollute the atmosphere between us.

Gayle's reaction was, "Yes, I've been noticing them too, but I think it's easier for a woman to stare than a man." We talked about the uselessness of guilt and other helpful concepts, but suddenly she said, "You won't believe what's coming down the beach! You've got to see this." At the time we were sitting up near the dunes, and Gayle, who has 20-10 vision, told me to get my glasses, took my hand, and led me down to the beach. "I'll put my back to her, and you look over my shoulder. We'll pretend to be talking."

And for the remainder of our stay, wherever we were, Gayle would point out fascinating bodies of all ages and sex and we had enormous fun discussing the highly unusual collection of shapes and nationalities on those islands. As you would expect, my guilt lessened and no harmful dynamic developed.

It just so happens that Gayle has always found body types very interesting and has never felt the slightest degree of guilt about this. Most men and women have learned a different attitude, and therefore the dynamic of one partner guiltily looking and the other angrily complaining or sullenly withdrawing is extremely common, especially when it is backed by a history of wavering commitment. For these couples, Gayle's solution would be forced and ineffectual. We will be discussing ways to dissolve patterns, but the point we wish to emphasize here is that participation occurs in the *feeling* of upset and that no blame is assignable because individuals cannot help feeling the way they do. Their attitudes were fed them along with the mashed carrots and watered-down applesauce. And even though it is true that the attitudes continue with their permission, realistically, permission cannot be withdrawn without sustained effort.

Insight: A Gift or a Weapon?

If the premise can be accepted that both participate, and if the couple can do this without measuring the *amount* of participation, a start has definitely been made, and the next step—that of coming together to lift the problem out of the relationship's way—can very pleasantly be taken. This, however, will not be done without resistance. If one partner wishes to bring something up, say, for instance, that the other becomes depressed and irritable when the guests have gone home and cleanup has begun, it must be understood that it is the instinct of all of us to feel attacked when another person singles out our behavior in any terms but praise. This is because we think we *are* our behavior, even though the concept is as insane as saying that we are the English language if that is what we grew up speaking. As children, we are schooled in certain traits and moods but we do not become them in any deep sense. Nevertheless, we do identify with them until such time as we choose to consult our hearts. Thus it is vital that each person try extremely hard not to become so defensive that access to the heart is blocked.

After the initial period of romantic euphoria is over and a little time has passed in relative clear-mindedness, most couples quickly develop a fairly accurate picture of each other's ego. The ego, which is the individual's collection of past experiences, cannot be camouflaged indefinitely and the honeymoon collapses, in a sense, from the exhaustion of pretense. Although this spells the beginning of more open conflict, as each partner observes the other's conditioning, they move into a position where they can now be of enormous help to one another.

Yet as you know, this is seldom the outcome, because instead of using their knowledge to help and comfort, it is usually employed as a weapon. During disagreements great and small, surprising skill is exhibited by both in going straight to the other's weakness. Over and over the blind areas are hit, and through the months and years a friend is gradually turned into a stranger.

We are all familiar with the many passing comments couples make in public about each other's sexual ineptitudes, lack of cooking skills, stinginess, tardiness, physical deficiencies, and other areas of sensitivity. Couples kid, complain, interrupt, and correct each other in a sad attempt to vent old angers and redress grievances, but please note that these attacks are not at random. Each knows well the weaknesses that the other does not wish exposed, and those of course are the ones most joked about.

If only we could experience pleasure of another sort—that which comes from protecting our partner's happiness in vulnerable situations, and then using only in private our good intuitions for good ends. Revenge, no matter how mild or humorously disguised, is not satisfying. Neither is there any fulfillment in clutching one's threadbare scraps of personality when what they hide is splendor.

Neither Bait nor Rise to the Bait

Our tired and bloodied ideal that every perceived attack must be met with counterattack needs to be reappraised honestly. This ancient habit can be dropped, and it should be the first bit of conditioning to go so that the other person's insights can be received. Defensiveness is not practical because only an illusion of oneself is being guarded.

Why attempt to protect a part of yourself you do not want? If you are angry you can be certain this is occurring, since the anger arises from feelings of self-betrayal. Therefore receive willingly any insight your partner brings you. Listen to it profoundly. Be not quick to close your mind merely because you discover some flaw in what is said. And do not brood on it later. All this will be harder at first than you may anticipate, but if you persist you will surely learn to protect instead your willingness to grow.

On the other side, the one who wishes to share what he or she has observed should follow certain commonsense guidelines similar to those used in resolving issues. (1) Do not make references to your partner's behavior when either of you is irritated. The hand must be open to receive. So wait for a mood between you that is somewhat supportive of such efforts. (2) Remember that it is also difficult for you to receive peacefully what your past has taught you is an attack. Thus you wish to be clear beforehand that you are going to be very accepting of your partner's reactions throughout the time of your attempted communication. (3) Treat the subject with respect and importance. Do not refer to his or her patterns flippantly or when circumstances do not allow for adequate concentration. Perhaps suggest that you both sit down, or let there be an understanding between you of how this kind of subject is to be broached. (4) Be very gentle in your approach. Your friend is doing the best he or she can. Therefore, use your store of knowledge wisely and kindly. (5) Speak in language that can be heard. Do not hold back making gestures, physically or verbally, that could help your partner be more receptive. Be understanding and willing to wait for his or her defensiveness to pass.

The practice that is being suggested here is difficult to master, not because it is hard to understand but because of our entrenched belief that any personal reference must either inflate us or damage us. That it could be for neither purpose, but instead for the aim of promoting friendship, seems improbable to the selfish side of us. Evidence for love can be felt only in the present, and the ego, being centered in the past, does not believe in love and thinks that anything done in love's name is a subterfuge. This, then, is what you are up against in both of you. So grudge not the gentleness with which you will have to introduce this practice. You are learning to trust what your partner sees about you, and in the past this has been used only to injure you, so naturally you are leery, as is your partner.

Despite your and your partner's good intentions, you must also be prepared for some degree of attack occurring during these sessions. You must expect this and not be thrown by it. Simply do your best to move past this age-old reflex.

The Symptom of Feeling Separate

To this point we have discussed the step of each party assuming his or her full participation in the creation of any dynamic, and we have suggested as the second step how each person's knowledge of the other's ego might be communicated. Now we come to tracing the antecedents of the disturbance, and, once again, the temptation will be to balance blame. The mind begins searching for counterexamples instead of earnestly considering what is being said: "Not only is what you say about me not true, but you do this other thing that is much worse."

If the couple can somehow accept that one ego is no better than another—which is a truth applying to all egos—then the step-by-step gain that can be so pleasant and rewarding has a chance of occurring. Unless you can move past the consideration of who has the most problems and finally understand that all problems are the *relationship's,* there is no real chance of these sessions helping. Think of them as periods in which you will practice being defenseless, and notice the simple rule that when you defend yourself you feel attacked, but when you relax and welcome help in any form, you feel safe and assured of the eventual outcome.

In a long-term relationship each person's patterns of mood and behavior will tend to trigger a reciprocal pattern in the other and dynamics are created that seem like strange, invulnerable entities that have joined the relationship. A few typical examples are:

> One makes occasional large purchases. The other makes frequent small ones. Both spend more money than the relationship has and blame each other for the results.
> One looks down on the other (socially, intellectually, physically). The other reacts in resignation or petty assertiveness. Both have yet to see what their partner is at heart.
> One is "loyal" (possessive and jealous), the other is "outgoing and friendly" (manipulative). Neither is a real friend to anyone.
> One is "consistent" (rigid) with the children. The other is "generous" (fearful) with them. As husband and wife, they fail to teach the lesson of unity and love.
> One is not committed to the relationship. The other

anxiously awaits abandonment. Neither has learned the meaning of trust.

Notice that in all these examples the outcome is some form of separation. The ego side of us believes that closeness threatens its specialness and naturally seeks to be split off. But this desire must be fed or it will die of its own nonsense. As we use the term in this book, every "dynamic" sets up a situation in which both parties feel justified in stepping back from the other. They play off one another's unhappiness and weakness, fanning the urge in each other to be apart. Thus you will always know when a dynamic is occurring by the feelings of estrangement and disparity it causes to grow within you.

"You Are Never Upset for the Reason You Think"

Although many steps led to the formation of each dynamic and often many steps are needed to undo it, abandoning the relationship altogether and starting "fresh" with another individual will not cut short the needed work, because the attitudes that contributed to the first set of dynamics are brought with you and although they will combine with different reactions from your new partner, the resulting blocks to love will be equally strong. There are good reasons for divorce, but having too many settled patterns is not one of them. The unhappy games that mar your present relationship are—of all opportunities on this earth—the greatest you have for personal growth and happiness.

All dynamics are the coming together of two weaknesses in education that join within the familiarity of darkness and dance a dirge to friendship. Learn to listen for the death rattle of these patterns, these familiar spirals into fear, anger and judgment. They are not difficult to recognize but recognize them you must, and then one of you can suggest, at an appropriate time, and in the wise and gentle way we have discussed, that work begin.

If one session is not sufficient and the pattern keeps repeating (a visit from certain acquaintances leaves one spouse feeling shunned as usual; sexual overture once again leads to emotional withdrawal; unexpected bills cause replay of arguments about the future), then a little program of ongoing efforts can be worked out that might include, for example, a brief period of joining before the in-laws arrive, before sex, before Saturday-afternoon TV, before the checkbook is balanced, or whatever seems to be the pattern-triggering circumstance, as well as a formal time of in-depth work once a day, twice a day—something that seems adequate and is agreeable to both.

During these sessions you wish to go beyond the surface layer of emotions. Usually the literal content of the argument (silent or overt) is irrelevant to the dynamic you want to reach. In fact, *a common symptom of all dynamics is that the upset is out of proportion to the incident.* Therefore, the thoughts and emotions encircling the immediate subject of attention must be gently parted so that the pattern behind them can be seen.

For example, if the upset is over money, one spouse might feel that the purchase in question was justified and the other that it was not, but neither is really upset over that or even over the history of purchases within their relationship. This can be very hard to see at the time, and consequently it is often good to wait awhile—hours or even days—before trying to get at the root.

Great discipline is needed not to return to the superficial during your dynamic-tracing sessions. The temptation will be to make one last point about the purchase, and perhaps that issue should first be formally resolved (Chapter VI), but remember that to stay stuck on the first level of perception leaves the dynamic untouched.

In our example, the most obvious feelings might be indignation, or possibly guilt, on the part of the one who did the buying, and anger or righteousness, perhaps even pity, on the part of the accuser. Yet below these are another set of attitudes. In this case let us make the purchaser a man and say that his *root* feeling is one of judgment. Specifically, he looks down on women in the area of finance. He believes it is the husband's prerogative to buy what he thinks best and that a wife should not question him. Women do not have financial aptitude nor is managing money their role. And let us say that the woman's root attitude is also one of judgment. She looks down on men who are not good providers. The job market is male dominated and there is no excuse for a man not to succeed in it. She believes that their family has inadequate funds and it is a husband's role to see that this does not happen.

Identifying the Problem's Veneer

As you sit together, the specific argument laid aside and your mutual purpose clearly in mind, you might begin by trying to describe the *similarities* within the many past incidents over purchases. Anything that could help keep this part of the discussion impersonal should be considered. For instance, the characteristics of the pattern could be written down, each point being agreed on, as if a joint report to a third party were being prepared. You could even pretend that you were consultants who had been hired by another couple—any device at all that will remind you that now the time has come to cease trying to correct each other and to look instead at the dynamic as a parasite on the relationship which both wish to eradicate.

Your description should include every typical emotion, thought, and outward occurrence that the two of you can identify. Possibly in the course of your analysis you will observe that the pattern always begins earlier than at the argument stage. Let's take as an example the dynamic of errands (involving groceries, car repairs, etc.) falling to one spouse more than the other and yet that one always feeling criticized for how the errands are done. During your review you discover that as this individual prepares to leave, certain parting words are common from the other (e.g., "Remember the budget," or "This time don't forget to buy ginger root," or "Just get whichever one you think best, dear," coupled with a few suggestions given and withdrawn in the same breath).

You discover that as the spouse sets out, he or she feels distrusted, somewhat friendless and inadequate, and vaguely excited over the idea of getting away and spending money.

The remaining spouse feels distrustful and seems genuinely perplexed as to what to do about his or her partner's obtuseness. Also noticed are tinges of anger and excitement over the prospect of being right.

The stages of making the purchases, the drive home, the typical way the argument begins and ends, and the like, would also be outlined, until the two of you reach a sense of thoroughness concerning all that can be seen about the veneer of the problem. Every opinion and observation need not become another issue in itself because absolute accuracy is never the goal. You merely wish to obtain a more specific sense of how this pattern plays itself out and to achieve a feeling of objectivity or distance between it and the relationship.

The Promise Sustains the Pain

Having done this much, you will notice that the dynamic is always like a plant: dark roots reaching down into the shadows of the past, shoots green with promise extending into the future. The greenery is the expectation that *this time* the dynamic will work. This time spending money will leave one feeling quenched, having an affair will end happily, striking one's partner will eradicate the intolerable behavior, drinking to excess will bring rest, staying away from home will bring peace. Even the smallest pattern of disturbance has its green component *for both partners,* or else it could not be sustained. There might not be—and usually there is never—any true reward, but be certain there is the hope of one and look carefully for it. These insights you wish to give and receive like keys to your separate chains.

You will tend to see each other more clearly than you see

yourself. Therefore, what do you suspect your participation offers you and what do you *see* is the gain that your partner seeks? Both of you must strive for utter defenselessness in order to permit this degree of honesty to surface, and the one offering the insight into the other's participation must be absolutely sure that he or she feels no judgment, even faintly. If you need to stop often to remember your objective of helping the friendship, of building a great love, then stop often. The dynamic simply cannot die until its life-giving expectations have been plainly and compassionately looked at. And conversely, any problem, once it is seen honestly, is ninety percent destroyed.

Most people are aware of their own personal dynamics, but they resist strongly looking at the origins of these patterns because of the hope of fulfillment they still cherish. Although these expectations may feel vital and alive to you and an exciting part of the present, they are in fact as dead as the soil from which they rise. They were given at the same time the attitudes themselves were taught and are as false a friend to you as they were to those who peopled your formative years. See this clearly and then take up the work of patiently tracing the dark roots of the problem as far back as you can reach. Here again, your partner can often see with less distortion, even into *your* own past. So do not be afraid to receive help from your best friend. Why defend an illusion that is preventing the one thing in life you want?

Stay Focused on a Single Thread

It is best to limit your efforts to the one problem area you are considering and not to bring in related dynamics. One modus operandi of resistance is to so enlarge the definition of an ego trait that it becomes lost in its own correlatives. If you are considering affairs, do not bring in masturbation merely because it too has a sexual element. If you are considering a tendency to talk against your spouse in public, do not add bragging simply because both require an audience. Likewise, being tight and miserly need not be linked to a history of getting fired, or taking too long to get dressed linked to fear of compliments. All things are of course connected, but the kind of lumping together that amounts to resistance is based on the belief that some connections are meaningful while others are not and that you are in a position to know the difference. If you will look carefully you will see that the usual reason for bringing in side issues is to make yourself or your partner feel guilty. And guilt is always a form of resistance. It is never necessary to pursue a line of thought that merely raises more questions and increases despair.

Begin with the dynamic as it is today, then look together at how it was expressed in recent days, and continue, very patiently and gently, trailing it back through time, relying heavily on each other's insights. Attempt to take it back as deeply into childhood as possible, but if at any time this seems forced, do not indulge in mere speculation. You are trying to *see,* not to reason. For instance, to consider diet during your mother's pregnancy, birth traumas, astrological influences at conception, and past lives will not provide truly usable insights for most people. You need no special knowledge to facilitate love, because love is the natural atmosphere of your relationship and will rush back into it at the slightest show of willingness. Be grounded, simple, straightforward, and intelligent. Whatever you know for certain about your own history is more than enough once it is honestly and innocently seen.

Observe how the attitudes you are tracing were expressed by your parents and other members of your family. Look at the times you grew up in. If your partner knows any of the principal actors in your formative years, he or she will probably be able to see in them the origins of this dynamic more plainly than you can.

Your goal is not formal proof. And emphatically it is not to pass judgment on your parents or anyone else. You wish only to see where these reactions come from so that you will know they definitely do not come from your heart, and thus you owe them nothing. It takes great self-awareness to realize that every lingering emotion, every recurring thought, does not have to be taken personally.

At this point we are mostly fake. Virtually nothing of what we think and feel has any deep meaning. It is almost better to start over, and if you can, do so. Start with your heart, your love, and peace, and forget the rest. If this is not possible, as for most of us it is not, be content to untie the knots of illusion one by one. It is good work that pays off in undisguised happiness. You like how you feel when you forgive. You do not like how you feel when you judge. What could be firmer ground to tread than this?

You must be meticulous in carrying out your self-probings free of censure. A good therapist lays bare the past so that it can be seen in innocence, and you wish to do no less for yourself and your partner. If the past is looked at with anger, it has not yet been fully seen. Attack thoughts are only possible when perception is still too shallow to dissipate them. Therefore do not encourage anger in yourself or your partner. You could only be angry at your parents for teaching a certain attitude if you still believe that attitude is your identity. And you could only be angry at yourself for reacting to life in predictable terms if you still have not seen that your reactions had a beginning.

A Brief Case History

As a general illustration of the tracing process we are recommending, let us consider the common dynamic in which one partner, usually the husband, wants less verbal communication, and the wife wants more. Gayle and I have seen very few relationships that did not include some variety of this pattern, but a few years back we worked with a couple for whom this was the major impasse and, according to them, their only incompatibility of consequence. It had developed shortly after they married and had endured for eight years.

The issue included conversations in general—she wanting more, he less—as well as talking things out—she believing this possible, he thinking that silence could clear the air—and so their dynamic was broad enough that their case serves as a good representation of what usually occurs. Here, first, is a summary of how they initially stated their positions to us:

Perhaps his attitude on conversing is best illustrated by his comment: "No one has ever taken a vow of chatter." And hers by this statement: "I married him because he seemed sensitive and intelligent, someone I could talk to. I had never gone out with a man I could really talk to and we talked quite a lot before we got married. Why should marriage change that?"

His answer was that of course they talked more, they were learning about each other. "Conversation is a tool," he said, "like a Phillips screwdriver. You don't use it on nails and bolts, you use it on a Phillips screw."

As a means of solving their problems individually, her position was that she could sense when he was in a state but she did not know whether the state concerned her, their marriage, their children, or what. If he would be more forthcoming when she asked him what was wrong, then at least her imagination would not feed on it, and he would benefit by getting it out.

His argument was essentially that many problems go away of themselves and those that do not could be worked out more quickly and effectively by himself. If a problem truly concerned her he would bring it up, but he had noticed that she tended to take anything he said personally and to blow it out of proportion. Consequently, he had learned to keep his mouth shut.

On resolving issues between them, she said that her husband would talk but not listen. If the discussion lasted longer than he thought it should, he would get angry and have nothing further to do with her. If she continued to bring it up, he was capable of shutting her out emotionally and sexually for days.

He told us that he did believe that some mutual issues could be talked through but that many of the subjects his wife centered on were either petty or short-lived. He said she seemed to believe that everything had to be settled in one sitting and tended to bring things up at the most inconvenient times "as some sort of test." When the discussion stopped going anywhere, he stated that, yes, he would indeed refuse to continue.

These, very briefly, were their ego positions when they came to us, and as you can see, there is no way of reconciling them without someone backing down. We started by having them carry pocket notebooks to record thoughts and feelings that seemed in any way connected to the dynamic. At the end of each week we would review together what they had observed. Three weeks of this brought forth a new set of insights and beliefs that lay just behind the old.

The woman's first insight was that whereas she had felt guilty about assuming that "his moods" always concerned her, it was actually a fear and not an assumption. Seeing this allowed her to switch from "I am paranoid" to the more accessible "I am afraid." Reading over the list of ideas she had caught herself thinking, she saw that her fear was "a tree with several branches." It was clear that she was afraid that she was stupid and shallow for wanting to talk, but also felt an angry resolve to prove—through getting her husband to take her seriously—that she was not. The insight here was that she had two conflicting attitudes that kept her in a bind: (1) talking was a sign of her being inane, and (2) talking had to be the means by which she received confirmation that she was worthy and appreciated.

Another branch of the tree was her fear that by not keeping her husband talking, she was failing to "hold her man." His silence was a sign that the marriage was falling apart. Her notebook also uncovered her concern that he was talking to someone else and that she "had a pretty good idea who."

Looking at this thought calmly, she realized that she was not at all sure he was talking to anyone and that the person she had in mind was actually a very unlikely individual for him to confide in. (He answered that in fact he had never "passed two words with her.")

Although she may not have been initially intuitive about her husband's feelings toward this other woman, good intuitions are often caught through watching the mind in this way. One that Gayle and I believed was quite accurate was her feeling that her husband's habit of silence was not making him happy and that "he would feel so much better if he could chat." And in the years that have followed, this appears to be what has developed.

The husband's notebook showed that he had a strong dislike of discussing his problems with anyone and especially looked down on the practice of a husband and wife resolving issues verbally. He was surprised by the depth of his feeling against this and noticed that an adult he had known as a teenager kept coming to mind. This was a man who was very much respected by the men around him. He was tall, good-looking but "not overly handsome," knowledgeable and very competent. He was not aloof but he did keep his own counsel. He never bragged, never gossiped; in fact, he seldom entered into conversations at all, but when he spoke, others listened. The husband interpreted this memory as meaning that his own stand was based more on wanting to *appear* manly (fearing to appear womanly) than on a reasoned-out internal value.

A related feeling that surfaced in the notebook was that his wife was forcing him to talk about his difficulties "too soon," and that by relenting, he was not giving himself time to work things out but instead was "running to mama." It was also clear that he did not expect his wife to really be able to help. In his opinion, she did not understand in any deep sense what he was saying and was too quick with advice.

He, too, recognized certain fears. One was that if they started a discussion, it would never end but would escalate into misunderstandings, hysterics and all-night arguments, or would simply drag on pointlessly and miserably. Very seldom had either of these things happened over the eight years they had been married, but his concern was that they would be frequent occurrences if he were to suddenly become more talkative.

He was interested to discover that he also feared a certain loss of identity. The feeling was that if he talked a great deal more to her, whether about issues or in general, he would become somewhat "weak and directionless." His mind would be less focused, more cluttered. He could see that this "catastrophic expectation" was not warranted, and this strengthened his recognition that there must be more at work behind his stand than common sense or mere personal preference.

Next we began helping this couple trace their attitudes back through earlier times and whenever possible into their childhood conditioning. Mainly our role was to help them not overlook important periods (a previous marriage, earlier jobs, schooldays, etc.) and, when childhood was reached, especially to help them keep clear the distinction between their parents' attitudes and how they chose to act them out. For example, the woman was able to see that her feeling that her husband's silences meant he was slipping away from her came in part from her early training that a girl must ask her date questions, get him talking about himself, and keep him interested. If he became silent and morose, it meant he would not ask her out again. Yet behind this were attitudes taught even earlier: If a man doesn't like you, it is your fault. And if a man doesn't like you, you are valueless. These beliefs can be acted on in many ways. Her mother had expressed them by cruelly deriding her father for his silence, probably because she had given up on him. Her daughter, however, never made fun of her husband and therefore assumed she did not have her mother's attitude. But when she remembered how her mother related to other men, especially one she was being introduced to, she recalled that she was "very male oriented" and would always shower the man with compliments and was obviously very desirous of being liked by him.

Likewise the husband at first did not see the origin of the attitude behind his silence in his father's example, because his father talked freely. But he talked at, not with, his mother. He did not respect her opinion on anything and obviously would never have confided in her or sought her help with personal problems. Issues were solved by his decree, and his mother, "a pretty little chatterbox," always went along.

Gayle and I worked with this couple for almost a year, and by the end of this time they had a sharp sense of their ego feelings (those absorbed during the formative years) in contrast to their true feelings. By recognizing that their partner's reactions were not deeply premeditated, they could forgive more easily and help more readily. They devised a plan that took each other where they were and emphasized gradual progress.

She learned that to push her husband to talk caused a strengthening of the very reaction she disliked. He learned if he truly wanted quiet to say so without withdrawing emotionally, and she in turn would respect this without reading anything sinister into it. As he began practicing what he came to call "divine gossip," he discovered that his wife was quite insightful and could indeed be of immense help to him personally. Furthermore he realized that she genuinely *liked* to talk, and he saw that there was nothing degrading in his giving her this pleasure often. When he finally looked at her honestly he could see that she simply was not a shallow or judgmental person, and so his fear that this kind of talk would pollute his state of mind was groundless.

One Underlying Dynamic

During most people's formative years an ideal of how life should be is set into place and thereafter is never relinquished. It remains in the background, an impossible standard that no relationship or circumstance can quite live up to. As a consequence, *nothing* is committed to with all the heart because it does not compare. This shuttling of the mind between the way one's life is and the way the little picture says it should be is largely unconscious. Thus discontent, whether it leans toward anger or sadness, is precious because it is the tip of the iceberg that reaches down to this "ideal of youth." If the discontent is admitted and looked at and if it is patiently traced back, then the ideal it leads to can be uncovered and in the light of common sense it will vanish, because, being purely of the ego, it is always an illogical and unworkable approach to the present.

One of my parents had a strong yearning for physical isolation and the other came from a family whose driving force was a belief in their absolute superiority. The picture of how my life should be that formed as a consequence was that I must be sought after but unavailable, an important and revered figure who lived alone and pursued those things the world was too backward to understand. From time to time I would attempt to act this out in various ways but always with unhappy results. During the stretches in between I was merely discontent with my life situation, whatever it was.

The last way this dynamic surfaced, before I recognized the real problem and with Gayle's help eliminated it, was in the form of a fantasy life fed by a series of novels written by an author who, I later realized, was portraying a similar ideal. By that time in life I had run through enough overt attempts to be superior or isolated that I no longer wanted to try others, but the ideal itself was still in the shadows, and it took the jolt of realizing I had withdrawn into a fantasy life, something I had never done before, to set me to work on digging out the remnants of this immature standard.

The phenomenon we are speaking of here has of course been described by many other authors. The essential point to understand is that very often there is a central dynamic underlying all the others. And it will gradually become obvious as you trace back the individual patterns of disturbance. A great deal does not have to be made of this concept, and certainly you do not want to torture each other by speculating on the identity of this hypothetical keystone to your ego. If you keep stumbling over it, then deal with it; if not, be assured that every small gain weakens the superstructure of your unhappiness and that it will collapse naturally if you persist.

You are dealing with an illusion of self and not a power. All you wish is to recognize your true feelings and beliefs, and there are countless paths to awareness. If the concept of a central dynamic does not seem timely, then begin with a problem at hand and work for practical relief. One's goal should always be kindness and not mentionable results.

Symbols of Your Sincerity

Although these retracing sessions will be quite effective by themselves, your progress will eventually be blocked if you do not follow through as consistently as you possibly can. For so very long you and I have proceeded through life blindly, looking at others and seeing nothing true, reacting blindly—blind to our own thoughts, our own sources of upset. Yet we can learn, and indeed must learn, how to live consciously. The formal periods of describing and tracking down specific dynamics mark the beginning of a conscious relationship in which the split between the ego, which cannot join, and the heart, which can, becomes more distinguishable. All you have to do is *see* the difference and your choice is made. No one remains imprisoned in misery once escape is recognized as simple and safe. Your escape from hate in any form is as elementary as a shift in attention. You love your partner or you love your history. You look to the peace of your heart to guide you or you look to your past. This is the choice we all make with each passing instant. Yet if you cannot distinguish between smallness and love, a change in mental focus remains impossible.

Thus the necessity of supplementing your sessions with continued efforts to become more aware of what is currently passing for thinking. If carrying a pad of paper and recording certain lines of thought helps to clear the mental muddle, then follow through in this way. If physically stopping frequently during the day and looking deeply into your heart for your true feelings helps you to recognize that the past is over and you are free, then follow through in this way. If formally practicing attitudes and behaviors that bring an increased sense of closeness between you and your partner undercuts the desire to be separate, then follow through in this way.

Watch also the little conversations. To forgive means to release, and you can be sure you have not released yourself from your past if you still talk against or joke about your parents. Hatred is an absolute glue. But it can be dissolved with awareness. Be conscious of any dark snatches of childhood memory, of unhappy reactions to parental phone calls, of anxiety over upcoming visits. Be honest with yourself. You know whether you have completed this work of seeing that your parents did the best they could. They tried hard, and of course they made mistakes—but you have not been damaged because you *can* still choose not to be.

Be conscious also of not passing the old family attitudes on to your children. Do your best in this. And whenever you slip, remember that you will not reform yourself through regret. A mistake calls only for correction. Release lies in seeing within you where the attitude originates and then drawing closer to another part. If your parents disciplined out of their mood, if as a child you never knew what to expect, do not strive to give your children the *appearance* of consistency. Rather, look deep enough to see what emotions are yours that are themselves consistent. Do you love your children? Then love is a part of you that is consistently available.

Above all, stay sharply aware of your thoughts and feelings about each other. Sort them out as carefully as you find shoes that fit you in a store filled with ones that do not. If your minds are choked with outgrown lessons, each generating some conflicting emotion, remember that the whole lot can be thrown out if the discarding is done with the one mood you wish to retain.

Be very gentle with each other. Rush is always of the ego. Learn to move quickly through the layers of the mind without rushing. And judge not your progress. Judgment is a shoe that no longer fits. Now you wish a great love, an enduring friendship, and this is won only with humility and an easy patience. Assume the position of the heart, for it is *your* heart. Nothing real about you has to be forced or molded or renovated. You are discarding mere fantasy, mere ego identities, and like imaginary playmates, they will fade as true companionship with your real friend is practiced and experienced.

CHAPTER VIII

Common Problems

One Problem—One Answer

In a counseling session there is always that moment when the pleasantries are over and it is time to get down to work. The therapist says, "Okay, now tell me what the problem is," or some such opener, and the couple look at each other to see who will go first. Then one of them begins his or her list of complaints, being careful to sound reasonable, but always there is at least a faint undertone of shock and disbelief. This is quite sincere because most couples think their problems are unusual, that somehow they have turned up with a spouse who afflicts them as no normal human would. And it is this same tone of startled outrage that most of their friends have given them as their way of showing support. If what one heard were all one knew of marital difficulties, the apparent conclusion would be that the pain of the problem is caused by its uniqueness and that as long as a problem is unusual, it is reasonable to take revenge on one's spouse.

Whenever a limitation is perceived as universal it is ranked as a mere inconvenience and not reason for the couple to fight. Thus many of the difficulties accompanying marriage are not classified as problems and consequently cause little dissension. In these areas the individuals simply accept the hardships, large or small, caused by the presence of another body. In other words, in these areas they accept their spouse.

Most couples take in stride having another person's furnishings and knickknacks taking up space around them, eating the same food for dinner, picking up the other's mail along with their own, having to share closet, drawer and refrigerator space. Some also divide household duties without issue and do not mind cleaning up after another person. One spouse may have a sensitivity to noise and so the other easily agrees to give up a downstairs apartment for an upstairs one. One may have an allergy to cats and the other also lives without them and does not think to question this. There are those who choose not to drink because of the difficulty this might cause their spouse who has a problem with alcohol. And even within the specific areas we will talk of later, there are couples who accept and accommodate each other without resentment. They live happily with the fact that now there are two sets of needs but only one income; there are two bodies but only one sexual act; there are two backgrounds but only one decision concerning their child is possible.

Eventually a couple must learn that all problems are the same and call for a common solution. The problem is always the potential for distance and separation and the answer is not to turn against each other. At first, however, their instinct will be the reverse—to look down on any perceived weakness in their partner. For example, a prevalent dynamic is that when one partner is afraid, the other reacts as though the fear were not reasonable or serious and tries to argue it away. Fear *is* an argument and cannot be relieved through counterarguments. The mind does not need more words. If we could just *look* at someone who is anxious we would know how to respond, and we would take the anxiety seriously because we take the person seriously. Fear in whatever guise is a plea for help, not for attack.

Likewise, censure does not inspire someone to be more financially responsible. Being criticized by the one whose affections he or she is afraid of losing will not make a jealous spouse less apprehensive. A husband who is impotent cannot be set free by becoming an object of pity or disgust in his wife's eyes. A wife's urge to chase after other men is not weakened by being met with anger at home. And to stop giving support to one's spouse does not make him or her a more caring parent.

These facts must become obvious if love is to extend throughout a relationship. The couple who wish to have real friendship train their minds to respond to all problems in the same way. Whatever it is, they view the difficulty as their joint responsibility and set forth together to calm the troubled area.

In our society a "problem" means someone has done something wrong and blame must be assigned. You wish to step away from this attitude because of its disastrous effect on friendship. Nothing is worth dividing over, even if the question *could* be answered in this manner. But the fact is that *to blame is to hold on to the problem.* The problem is *needed* as evidence of the other's guilt.

If one spouse is made out to be the cause, the difficulty is immediately brought into the heart of the marriage. It is attached to only one, and yet that person is half the friendship. The usual problem-solving method most couples use literally sacrifices the relationship to the problem, because no doubt is left in anyone's mind which is more important.

What you and your partner wish to do instead is to become like two scientists looking at an unfamiliar germ. Assume nothing about it except that it is smaller than the two of you. Discuss it and look at it as outside the bond between you, for truly it is. Make the problem the stranger and not each other. "What are we going to do about this little intruder? I am willing to try these things. What might you do and can you think of anything else I could try?" Thus the difficulty becomes a way of joining still further.

Throughout our marriage Gayle and I have had what we have come to call bad-toaster karma. Thus we know from repeated experience that when a toaster catches on fire, two sane people do not stand around trying to figure out who is most to blame. The house they live in is in danger and each rushes to put out the fire.

There is nothing abstruse about having a single approach to all troubles. The threat is always to your love and so more love is always the answer. Eliminating the germ, the fire, the financial or sexual difficulty is merely the means you use to extend love, to extend simple understanding and acceptance. Whose problem it seems *most* is irrelevant. What have you gained if you stand back and let the kitchen burn merely to teach your spouse a lesson?

It is still a problem if only one partner thinks it is—because unattended, it can pollute the relationship. Therefore waste not one instant judging the gravity of the difficulty. Throw away not one second of your relationship in trying to convince your partner that his or her concern is groundless. Isn't your friend in distress? The distress, then, is the problem, not the form it takes. Rush to relieve the distress, not to judge it.

Do not question the way a friend calls for help. "I am jealous!" is as good as "I am on fire!" "I feel threatened by our finances" is as good as "I feel threatened by someone at the door." Chase the stranger away even if you see no one there. Keep your eye on your partner's distress and continue helping until it is gone.

Unless you accept your friend's unhappiness as your own, you have indeed chosen to have no friend. Therefore choose again, and be each other's absolute buddy. This is the ancient and sacred answer to all relationship problems.

SEX

How's Your Sex Life?

No one even knows what "good sex" is. There is no trace of agreement on how frequently it ought to occur, what percentage of the activity should be devoted to foreplay, whether it should be planned or spontaneous, whether climaxes are necessary, if it is best if they are simultaneous, or from what part of the body they should arise. Some authorities recommend purely mental climaxes; others teach couples how to voluntarily abstain from sex altogether.

The little picture of ideal sex that is now in most people's minds—and therefore the level of sex they think they personally deserve—comes mostly from movies and adult TV. And these scenes are faked! Scientific descriptions are no more realistic, because words are not experience, even when composed by a lab technician. And most fiction is written to sell. That leaves perhaps the recollection of a time or two of pure ecstasy with some other person. But even if these memories were accurate, which because they are incomplete they are not, what we are considering here is a sex *life,* not a few isolated occasions on which our ego got most of what it wanted. A sex life, as the term implies, is a continuous thread, and whereas many people will claim some splendid moments, very few can state that they have ever known a happy sex life with anyone.

Many who are married would say that their spouse is a good or adequate cook, that they think well of their own contributions, and that on the whole they enjoy the meals they have together. Most couples have no real complaints in this area. But if the world turned its attention to good food the way it has to good sex, the fairly widespread satisfaction with this aspect of married life would vanish. Just imagine how ludicrously distorted the gentle pleasure of breaking bread would be if suddenly meals with the opposite sex were made out to be the greatest potential source of happiness and the only true basis of love. Soap operas would show just the bare beginnings of clandestine suppers. Movies would omit not even the dessert. Articles would appear on "How to Serve Him Pork en Croute" and exposing "The Desensitizing Effects of Broccoli on Taste Buds." Centerfolds would display sets of good teeth and list the models' favorite midnight snack. At the top of the bestseller lists would be books on *Chewing for Maximum Ecstasy* and *A 1001 Nocturnal Uses for Suet.* Public schools would ban cooking classes and alternative schools would offer courses on "How to Share Your First Banana." Studies would be published on *The Secret Life of Older Eaters,* and adolescents would be urged by their Sunday-school teachers to think twice before opening their lunch boxes "to just anyone."

Undoubtedly the effects on marriage would be similar to what taking sex out of context has produced. All would now think they were due a certain level of culinary excitement, and all would have strong but conflicting impressions of what that was and an unshakable conviction that whatever it was, it was not forthcoming in their relationship. And these new grounds for outrage would seem quite plausible. You meet, you fall in love, naturally you want to share your chicken croquettes. But, shock of your life, six months after you're married, your spouse turns vegetarian. How could anyone be happy married to a vegetable freak? If you can't share the main course, what's the point in being married?

Perhaps some readers are thinking, "Yes, but sex is different." And of course it is, but it does not follow that a sex life must meet certain criteria before an individual can feel happily married. Eating a meal with someone is not the same as sexual intercourse. Neither is talking together the same, and still there are couples who because of language barriers, physical handicaps or psychological blocks do not talk to each other, yet some of them are quite happy—happier perhaps than many couples who can converse with ease. Their happiness is not limited merely because this one avenue of communication is disturbed or nonexistent.

There are countless ways for two people to share and be together. Sex is just one of them. It is not, as it has been made out to be, an intrinsically better or more meaningful way. Talking together, walking together, eating together, going out together, playing with the baby together, sleeping together, driving together, entertaining together, having sexual intercourse together, and any of a thousand other ways of joining can at any time be singled out, burdened with expectations, and made into a little hell—but this is never necessary. And if it *has* been done it can be undone. Gayle and I know of several truly happy marriages in which the sex life would be wholly unacceptable to most of the married population. We know many couples who have worked hard and have turned what was before a very angry and disturbed activity into a pleasant and satisfying one. And we also know two marriages in which the people have decided to "just not mess with the whole subject" and have been quite happy for many years. They consciously overlook society's clamorings on this subject and have prepared creative answers for probing questions from friends. In all these cases the decision about what to do was arrived at jointly with each person's needs and wishes carefully weighed. This is always possible no matter how divergent the two positions seem at first.

Four Qualities Essential to Success

As we said at the beginning of this chapter, there is one problem and one solution. This approach can be surprisingly freeing to the couple who adopt it. There will never be an end to problems, and so the key to coming to peace with this major theme of married life is to focus on how to deal with problems together rather than on the uniqueness of the latest one. Eventually a couple can learn to pass lightly over each obstacle so that a sense of coasting rather than bumping along develops.

The first step in this process is learning to put the issue back into perspective and seeing it as less important than the relationship. It is simply one stone in the path, and although it is the one you have come to now, you will treat it like any other and join hands to walk around it. Therefore you should look carefully at how our society has taken sex out of context and at how, as would be expected, many couples have fallen into this trap. Before becoming alarmed, if you find that you and your partner are in that trap also, it is good to stop, look around, and then plan your way out.

Go deeply into your heart and observe that the media's fomentations over sex are not your feelings. When society singles out any subject for mass attention, it begins absorbing the emotions, values and insanities of society itself. Thus "good sex" is now linked with our preoccupation with youth, current styles in bodily appearance, super health and super stamina, special knowledge of technique, newness and differentness, and a number of other irrelevancies. You *can* see for yourself that the premise is false that sex is better with someone younger rather than older, someone new rather than the one who is well known, someone knowledgeable and proficient rather than a person of common skills. These values are based on scarcity. And certainly we can become very excited over the prospect of getting what we believe almost no one else has. Excitement, however, is not the same as happiness and its presence does not mean there will be an increase in physical pleasure; in fact, with intercourse it often works against it.

The trap we fall into when we accept these values is that we set both our own and our partner's esteem into decline. Comparing ours to the sensations we imagine others to be experiencing can cause us to fight and hate our bodies. Articles on how to be sexier send us off seeking an interminable goal. Our spouse does not remain new, young, different or forever in style. Neither can anyone we choose instead. Which means that to have the level of novelty and excitement that is currently the ideal, we must become a vampire who sucks people dry and discards them. This brutal mind set now constitutes much of what passes for relationships among singles and bleeds many marriages of all hope and trust. To traffic in bodies is a very unhappy way to live, as is any area of life in which we decide that we must become a taker in order to be satisfied.

However, you cannot expect these feelings, even if you do recognize their source, to disappear magically. It took time for you and your partner to develop your present attitudes and stands, and steps will be needed to return your reactions to normalcy. It is fine for sex to be a pleasant part of marriage, and if you so wish, this you may have. But be fair to your partner and to yourself about this. Do not cast each other as the deterrent to progress. So convinced are most people that they know exactly what they are due sexually that if they note their partner deviating in the least, they throw up their hands and say, "You are impossible."

Part of fairness includes being finished with the childish belief that if your spouse truly loved you, he or she would know what you want done to your body without ever being told. Please observe that even *you* don't know what you want done, that it constantly changes, that even when your partner follows your instructions impeccably, it still is not quite right. Even a sexual fantasy cannot be controlled absolutely. Be open with each other about your likes and dislikes, but also learn to rest your pleasure on something more charitable than a perfect pyramiding of sensations and sights.

Granted you would *like* foreplay, or intercourse, or your spouse's body, or the time of day, or some other component to be "better." It is also true that you would like the scenery to be better when you walk, the food better when you eat, the road conditions better when you drive. Perhaps you would prefer snowcapped peaks to municipally planned parks, Russian caviar to lumpfish, and deserted country lanes to expressways, but you are capable of considerable happiness nonetheless because you are not consumed with your rights and your own personal importance in these particular areas. You naturally exercise your inherent fairness and reasonableness. Perhaps your spouse's approach is awkward, the dismount isn't that of a gymnast, and in between it could never be said that he or she plays your body like a Stradivarius. Whatever the limitations may be, unless you use these times of relating sexually as the hallmark of your worth as an individual and the final indicator of the success of your marriage, they can unquestionably be filled with love and pleasure.

Your happiness as a couple is in the content and not the form of the activities you engage in. This principle is often clear at the start of a relationship, when two are more apt to look at each other with innocence. During this period of willingness great happiness can be experienced under very modest circumstances. In fact the simple, ordinary situation is often valued for its lack of interference with the true content of the relationship. And the weaknesses of the other person, even the sexual ones, are not taken as a personal affront but are often viewed as quaint or even part of that individual's charm. What changes as they go along is the couple's attitude toward giving. Although perhaps they did not realize it, they had a time limit on their unselfishness, especially in the area of sex.

Many can give of themselves for a moment or two, provided the adult or child they must deal with is like a doll that they can take up and put down at will, with no strong wishes of its own. But very few people give in a truly sustained manner. Yet it is precisely this kind of inner integrity that is often required to dissolve a sexual problem that seems to have become a separate force within the marriage.

Thousands of people—acceptable to their partners—have bodies and make moves that you would find far more intolerable than your own partner's. If you wish progress in this area you must come to see that conditions need not be totally gratifying or certain concessions won *before* you can once again commit yourself to trying. You are free to be empathetic whenever you choose. Your natural generosity is not tied to the behavior or appearance of anyone.

Observation and Options

These then are the tools with which you begin. Your perspective makes sex smaller than your relationship. Your fairness shows you that everything does not have to be the way your ego wants it within this one little area. Your willingness allows you to start over. And your innate unselfishness gives you the persistence to unravel what may be a very old and seemingly hopeless entanglement. As to the first overt steps you will take, this of course must be decided together and need not be dramatic. Often there is such heightened sensitivity and defensiveness in this area that it is good to have a plan that contains very small steps and to take each one gently and in peace.

A marriage counselor cannot be of complete help to a couple and still avoid considering their sexual relationship if that subject arises. And invariably it does. Having dealt with many marriages, Gayle and I have had to join with these couples in finding a way around a surprising variety of sexual problems. Needless to say, it would require a separate book to cover all of them, and in fact there are many helpful works dealing with the specific kinds of symptoms and dynamics that can arise. Our purpose here is merely to show that sex can be dealt with as a common problem rather than as an exception.

As with any difficulty, you wish first to look at it, to study it. Treat it as a separate entity outside your relationship and become curious about it. When does it happen? How does it begin? What emotion does it feed on? How does it usually end? Like an exotic pest that enters your backyard from time to time, you want to discover how this difficulty enters your relationship and how it behaves once it is there. You want to track its every move. What words and especially what thoughts precede it? Are there triggering events? Are there surrounding circumstances that affect it? All this *can* be done dispassionately, but you will have to work hard not to slip into blaming just a little, defending just a little, being remorseful just a little.

So do work hard and prove to yourselves that your relationship is capable of producing good joint effort.

Second, you want to be certain you are not limiting your options in any way. Perhaps the main reason sexual problems tend to set in and become inaccessible infections is that the couple is not considering hundreds of avenues open to them—and both partners participate in this. One effective means of broadening your scope is to have brainstorming sessions in which you make lists of possible solutions, beginning with ones that are absurd and off the wall and working down to more feasible alternatives. When you are making these lists, do not consider whether you would *want* to try something; just play a game of thinking of as many possibilities as you can.

Detailing the First Plan

Now you are ready to choose the particulars of your plan. Do not look at it as "the" solution but merely as the first thing you will try. Remember that there are countless ways around any difficulty, and you do not wish to delay relief by attempting to pick a perfect or superior way. Remember too that nothing you try is irrevocable; you are free to change your mind later. Neither is it possible that the step you take will solve all your sexual problems forever. A temporary improvement is all you seek, and if this does not transpire, you will simply sit down together and consider other alternatives.

For example, it is common for intercourse to be physically painful to one of the partners. And almost as common is the reluctance of couples who have this problem to consider using special lubricants, anesthetics, or dilators; reading books on the subject; doing research at the library; and other promising avenues. Or, these failing, to consider alternate forms of lovemaking, which could be very pleasant and satisfying if given a reasonable chance. But once again the couple is not open because they think life should be different for them. They deserve no sexual problems or only small familiar ones. Certainly they shouldn't be obliged to try devices, to study or to express their sexual urges in any but the old ways. Better to find a new playmate. Like two-year-olds, they do not understand why everything in the world cannot conform to their will.

In many long-term relationships the core problem is simply that lovemaking has become such an unhappy and conflicted event that it takes place very rarely if at all and this seeming failure weighs heavily on the couple. They cannot talk peacefully about the subject and feel they must be either dishonest or joke quite cruelly about it to others. Confessions are made to friends and time and again the partner is betrayed in these conversations.

When this dynamic is present it is sometimes easiest simply to start your sexual life over. Pretend you are living in the fifties and have just met. Or imagine you know absolutely nothing about sex, your own body, or the bodies of those of the opposite sex. You discover a manual for couples who are void of knowledge and you begin with the first section. This could be anything, but as an example it might be entitled "Locating the Nerves of Pleasure." Here it is pointed out that these nerve endings have been arranged differently in each body and can only be found through gentle experimentation. And so you and your spouse purchase, say, one of the large "Jeanie" type vibrating massagers that some chiropractors use (or a feather, a hot water bottle, a chamois glove, a good body oil, etc.) and one night a week, for twenty minutes only (or other precise days and time limits), with perhaps music or food and other things you both enjoy as part of the atmosphere, you begin helping each other explore your bodies for pleasant sensations, touching or massaging the other in turn in predecided ways and not requesting departures from the ground rules agreed to beforehand. *It is often advisable to omit the erotic areas in the first few "dates"* and to ease into what are thought of as the more sexual type of activities later and *very gradually,* what and when being decided together.

Often a highly formalized and rigidly structured beginning

like this can allow the couple to have, for the first time, one positive experience with each other's body. This is then built on step by step until a wider range of activities becomes possible.

In formulating your plans for dealing with your particular sexual difficulty, another option that can be considered is to look outside your own range of thoughts. If there is a chance that it would ease and quicken your way to go to a counselor you both can trust, then what is lost in making this effort? Many people, especially men but also some women because of their lingering sense of personal responsibility for all sexual problems, are reluctant to "admit failure" by seeking help. With everyone around them implying that they have such glorious sex lives, they believe they should be able to take care of this by themselves, and if by seeking another person's ideas it became apparent that they could not, they would be proved severely lacking, almost less than human. What the ego fails to see is that "taking responsibility" includes being open to help when help is needed.

Anyone who counsels couples can tell you that what are usually thought of as severe sexual difficulties are *likely* to arise in most long-term relationships. But even if you were the only two people who had not attained complete mastery, how could pride serve you? How can you be an actual friend if there are limits to your friendship? Of course friendship does not mean automatically granting every request another makes; it does, however, mean being open. Help from outside sources is only one of many roads past your problem, but it is one and therefore should be gently discussed between you and each person's fears carefully weighed. Then if one partner's feelings are still strongly against this, the other should be watchful not to add this issue to the problem.

In formulating your plan, do not make the mistake of imposing impossible rules on the relationship. There are no behavioral do's and don'ts that will chart a course free of all future difficulties. It is not as if a magical formula for all this were possible and somehow you must come up with it. For example, injunctions such as "never make love to me unless you really want to" presume a level of certainty that no one is capable of. Everyone is a little uncertain about everything. Who would say, "Don't take that next bite of squash unless your whole heart is in it"? If we took such a request seriously we would become hopelessly confused over whether we really want the next bite to be squash or Brussels sprouts? Is the squash a little soggy tonight? Didn't Mother tell us we hated squash as a child, or was that parsnips? Maybe we are actually full and are merely cleaning our plate from habit. . . . See the gesture *behind* the hug, the kiss, the pat. Obviously your partner is trying, even if imperfectly.

Do not rule out large areas of activity or set arbitrary limits on time and place, except temporarily to achieve a specific goal. Anything is okay if it is not harmful. Allow yourselves some latitude both together and apart. You are not perverted simply because you try things and act out fantasies. It is also fine to be very "straight" if this makes you happier. But if you can, avoid deciding everything from past experience. Perhaps you have changed. Perhaps something that is not particularly appealing to *you* would be an enormous gift to your partner. All happiness is not sensual. There is deep pleasure in giving and in being a friend.

Summary

We wish to stress again that sex is not love and it is not the core of a real relationship. It is merely an option that most choose to exercise. If it can be seen apart from the silly significance that it is presently being given, there is room enough within its tiny scope for enjoyment and love to abound. If, however, it is singled out by the couple as the weather vane of their affection, this little meeting place will fill with judgment. If it is regarded as the bounty due for the sacrifice of marriage, it will dispossess rather than bless.

Your sexual time together has no more potential for mystical union, transportation into rapture, enlightenment, or entering third or seventh heaven than any other moment of sharing. And as is abundantly apparent to many, its potential for misery is no less. Intercourse and all its spinoffs are wholly neutral. They do not constitute a separate force. They are neither negative nor positive, nor are they the essential reinforcements of a great love. And yet blame over sex can contaminate your entire relationship, just as blame can infect any form of communication.

Because of the undue attention it is currently receiving, people believe they must have strong opinions on sex and take rigid stands. You need no opinion on sex; you need take no stand. All you require is harmlessness and consideration. Let the madness roll off you. Let gentleness take its place. Use the tools that are available, such as the chapter in this book on resolving issues. Above all, do not lose hope and be set back by the least little failure, the slightest reminder of an unhappier time. You have observed and have learned how to be with each other easily in other situations. This need be no exception. It often takes great persistence to smooth out these very old patterns. But work is not humiliation. Far more than this one small area of your relationship will benefit from such an effort.

JEALOUSY AND TRUST

Jealousy's Counterpart

Jealousy has no external cause. It is self-contained. This does not make it one partner's problem more than the other's. We have said before that the ego has no real emotions, it only has reactions, and jealousy is undoubtedly a reaction, but it is not for that reason attributable to another's provocations. We are responsible for our reactions because we produce them. And when we so choose we can replace them. But in the case of jealousy this is especially hard to do by oneself because a jealous person is, for the moment at least, convinced that he or she is alone. Therefore never leave your partner alone to deal with jealousy. Do not turn away in disgust, for this will only make the argument on which jealousy is based more undeniable. Instead, treat your partner's pain as your own and be a true friend.

Jealousy is a surprisingly common dynamic. About half the couples who come to us suffer with some form of it. Yet despite its prevalence it is not considered chic at this time. To be "cool" is the ego emotion of preference. A casual, careless indifference to one's partner is now taken as a sign of great inner freedom, possibly even enlightenment. Being jealous is not being autonomous, and above all the ego cherishes autonomy.

It is essential to see that neither extreme provides an atmosphere in which friendship can flourish. Perhaps the days when women were advised to make their man jealous as a means of amplifying his ardor are behind us, but the premise of that psychology has not yet been seen through. It is still believed that jealousy is a power capable of manipulating love, only now in a negative direction. You are certainly free to love your partner less, but it will not be his or her jealousy that has caused you to do so.

Being Attractive

The ego side of us is incapable of friendship, yet it does have its substitute. It believes that to be wanted is to be loved. Accepting this thought as heartfelt, we experience an urge to let others know how special we are: especially earnest, especially well informed, especially gifted, especially beyond the sins of certain others we can name (and do name). Or recently we have been very sick. Very interesting or tragic things happen to us. And of course we also dress and hold ourselves to indicate our differences. Most people feel the impulse to get their specialness across the instant they start talking. They feel it in the morning as they select their clothes. And much of what they do throughout the day is to put in store little specialnesses that will later make them more "attractive" to others, or at least more respected.

The effect, however, is the reverse. We may perhaps succeed in making someone "value" us—meaning *want* to have us as a friend, lover, whatever—but we do not attain what we truly seek, which is genuine love. Telling people how special we are, however artfully done, separates rather than joins. "I am different from you," whether the world thinks those differences are negative or positive, does not lead to feelings of oneness. And this is no less true of the universal gambit of dressing and behaving so as to seem more desirable or available.

The way that the spouse who is "provoking" jealousy presents his or her specialness is sometimes very obvious. Yet it is this same specialness that the jealous mate is trying to keep as his or her own. Ironically it is of little use to either. Both, then, have a shared problem: they value the valueless.

Naturally there are people who behave pleasantly and dress pleasingly with no intent of "being attractive." The proof that they are genuinely uncalculating is in their willingness to modify their dress or actions in ways that will make life easier for their partner. Few, however, are open to considering such changes because, more than they want to be a friend, they care about the amount of chest hair showing, dropping innuendoes about their money or accomplishments, the jeans that fit "just right," the pat, the hug, the tilt of the head, the unblushing stare that makes them a little more apparent, a little more outstanding. And without greater honesty than most people are used to exercising, they cannot see why they should accommodate a jealous spouse.

Thus jealousy is no more "insane" than its counterpart, the unwillingness to accommodate. Both positions are difficult to relinquish, but it can be done—and without any real sacrifice.

The key, once again, is the couple's total commitment to friendship.

Pathological Jealousy

Certainly there are cases in which the spouse's jealousy is pathological, and no matter what change the other makes, it is never good enough. The most innocent of actions is grossly misinterpreted, and unfaithfulness is arbitrarily read into every gesture and word spoken. If this is true in your relationship, then you must come together, be open and gentle with each other, and realize that the effort before you will be more demanding than usual. You must proceed in an intelligent step-by-step manner, the same as with any other problem. You must hold each other dear and prove once again the power of a single purpose.

Needless to say, these pathologies are rare, yet the feeling on the part of those who have "normal" jealous partners can be quite similar because in their own minds they deny that they are "doing anything wrong." What they mean is that they see other men or women dressing and behaving the way they do and they don't understand why they can't just live their lives precisely how they wish and be obliged to no one. The answer is that such a life is indeed possible, but it is void of real relationships. In a real relationship it is a pleasure to ease the way for one's partner.

Trust Is Not Control

For his or her part, the jealous spouse must learn genuine trust. A partner has not been made reliable by being put "under control." *Never use your ego needs to dominate a situation.* To do so will only cause you to identify with them all the more strongly, and you already know that even a small degree of selfishness makes you unhappy. If you find that you are jealous, rather than asking yourself if the feeling is justified, simply go to your partner and ask for help. In so doing, be certain not to imply that your partner is somehow to blame. If the situation the two of you are in at the moment—at a party, in public, around a certain individual, or whatever the stimulus may be—is simply too difficult for you to handle, then obviously you and your partner should leave. But leave together, truly together, and take not with you blame of anyone or feelings of defeat and worthlessness.

You are expecting too much of yourself if you believe you should suddenly be immune to symbols that have called to your ego for a lifetime. Accept help or ask for help, but if your partner is not as cooperative as you would like, make a sustained effort to be fair while at the same time taking the steps you need to shelter your emotions during this period of healing.

Whenever possible, do not put yourself in circumstances that will "test" you. There will be tests enough without calling your ego out to fight. And if you find that you are losing your sense of peace and must break with the situation, then at least *try* to do so easily and happily even if you must do it alone.

When you attack another for not caring, you merely demonstrate your own lack of respect for care. Be a teacher of gentleness, for it is only through love that you will recognize that trust does not rest on what another's body does but on seeing the unchanging nature of the heart.

Specific Steps

There are many other ways jealousy can manifest itself: over one's partner's career, height, intelligence, popularity, income, humor, memory. Sometimes this will feel like "friendly competition" (the ego loves self-contradictory terms). Yet none of these varieties of ill will need frighten you. Begin as usual by studying the difficulty as if you were seeing it for the first time. What triggers it? A night out with the boys? Kidding and joking? Touching and hugging others in public? Using the word "I" and never the word "we"? What helps it dissipate? Staying physically near each other during trying situations? Checking in by phone? Being on time? Leaving unsaid what will obviously be misinterpreted? How does the jealousy feel? What thoughts precede it? What thoughts feed it? What *exactly* is your mind saying you should do when you are in one of these states?—murder? maim? run away? And what are your *true* feelings? And so forth, until you know the emotion so well that you can now chart your course around it quite easily, bringing all alternatives with you that could help.

Your Partner's Place in Your Mind

When one line of unhappy thought ends, the ego will always have another to take its place. This phenomenon can be clearly seen even in the course of a single day. The answer lies in learning how to reach quickly the level of the mind that knows peace. It is enough simply to interrupt the idea, whatever it may be now, to look at it and then return to an innocent acceptance of the present. How easily the mind returns to the present! To berate oneself is therefore unnecessary. As you come to know the part of you that is not selfish, you will also understand that your partner is similarly constructed. Trust is one continuous whole, whether trust that the partner who is jealous is not a misfit or trust that the one who seems to be causing the affliction is not truly an enemy. Take then this place that you occupy in each other's mind and remove the needles of judgment and holes of fear and gradually make it over into one fine bright place of welcome that heartens and blesses you and shines graciously on this one who walks beside you and calls you friend.

AFFAIRS

A Symbol and Its Effect

As we have said throughout this chapter, if two truly wish friendship, all problems between them are the same. Thus a circumstance that is a problem for one couple is not for another because it does not prompt them to stand apart. Although this is still true in the example of an affair, very few fail to see it as a problem, and for many it is the greatest tragedy and disgrace a marriage can suffer. The unthinkable has happened, and they curl up inside themselves and wrap their shock and shame around them or, worse, perhaps, seek repayment in pain, an open-ended penalty that will never be adequately paid.

An affair does not leave a scar on a relationship, but a scar can definitely be maintained in the mind. Like a jailer keeping guard over his prisoner, we cannot hold our partner in the past without remaining there also. If we want the mark of guilt to stay, we must be the living proof that the effects of his or her sin can still be seen.

Would you not rather turn from the past and teach innocence? Heal yourself quickly so you may show your partner that you have not been hurt and that you preserve no right to have darkness between you. If the circumstances were reversed would not such a friend be easier to walk forward with, one who teaches that the answer is more important than the mistake?

Unless it was a once-in-a-lifetime slip, the person who has affairs, or who habitually longs to, often needs much assistance to free his or her mind of this preoccupation, and this you wish to give in place of judgment. An affair is not a fatal sin and in some relationships it is not even a mistake, for undoubtedly there are couples who have an "open marriage" and place such little importance on the symbolism of sex that their devotion to each other never wavers. This, however, is not as easily done as many would like to believe, even though in the current climate those who try, either with or without their partner's concurrence, are now in the majority. Gayle and I have known at least twenty couples who have attempted to practice some form of open marriage, and in all instances the effects on their relationship were extremely unhappy. Most marriages simply will not survive this kind of experimentation, but that fact does not make it grounds for denunciation and attack.

Since this is a book for couples and since the chances are remote that any two would be reading it who could live together unaffected by the symbolism that having outside sexual partners would produce, we will address the subject as a problem and one that in many instances triggers considerable misery.

What Are You Going to Do About It?

Although unhappiness tends to accompany affairs, the unhappiness itself can be lessened if not eliminated *even though affairs continue.* Naturally, if they stop, the atmosphere can improve far more easily. You should be aware of the possibility that your partner may not be able to give these up for a long while, or having done so outwardly will still nurture the thought and mourn his or her missed opportunities, thus staying at a distance from you. Yet still it is possible for you to continue being a friend and to have a growing sense of peace during this period.

When an affair becomes apparent, the partner who has been betrayed—and in most relationships it is indeed meant and received as a betrayal—often feels a persistent compulsion to "do something about it." This urge is not from the heart and does not have to be interpreted or acted on. It is always your option to do nothing, and it may be beneficial to your relationship for you to take this position until you are very clear about what you want to do and why.

You will generally forfeit the opportunity to wait if you talk a great deal or at all to others about what has happened, because very few people genuinely see affairs as a neutral activity and therefore think they must give advice. The fact that they are not clear themselves will not mitigate the pressure of the implied request that most advice carries. They will want you to follow their suggestion out of respect for them and will tend to get angry when you hesitate. In addition to this pressure, *you may very well feel judged by those you have confided in,* because of the notion that if one were an adequate sexual partner these kinds of things would not happen. This is nonsense, of course, but it is still widely if unconsciously believed even by many who consider themselves freethinkers.

If there is one who is a true friend to the relationship and who you are certain can help you see the innocence of all those involved, then this kind of support can be sought without risk. A great many "supporters" are not needed, and you wish to watch closely the desire to be the innocent victim so beloved by all because of the villainy of your spouse. To find a mutual target, whether your own partner or the third person, will not draw friends to your side, even though this can appear to be the temporary effect. The ego experiences a false sense of closeness when a pact of hate has been formed, but these are never satisfying and are deeply disrupting to your peace.

The urge to "do something about it" can take many other forms besides desiring to inform others, and even this can seem a duty to be performed (e.g., your spouse's parents should be told because they have been so close to the two of you that you "owe" it to them). Questions of whether you should pack up and leave, begin divorce proceedings, also have an affair to balance the scale, seek out someone of the opposite sex to confide in because you are so alone in all this, threaten suicide, force a choice, and/or confront the other woman or man will tend to race around the mind, demanding action. Do not fight these thoughts; simply interrupt them and turn, over and over again, to the part of you that looks at all things in peace and knows what is truly in your best interests.

Making a Decision

If one way of responding seems more compelling than the rest, do not get caught up in deciding whether this course of action would be good or right or what the ramifications might be. You will never see what to do with calmness and certainty by analyzing, worrying and weighing alternatives. This is your ego trying to figure a way to get what it wants, and the reason this is such an anxious and conflicted activity is that on a deeper level you know it is not possible to foresee and control the future. You need another basis for your choice, and peace will provide it.

Focus on your state of mind and not on the question. Once your mind feels gentle and harmless, ask yourself what peaceful preference you have for this instant, for this day. Is there some first step you wish to take that could be carried through without conflict and that you would not think a great deal about afterward? If so, then act on it, and refuse to tell yourself where it is leading, because you truly do not know. Simply take this first step and then do not reconsider. Your state of mind was more reliable, more peaceful, steadier, when you made the decision than it is now that your ego is trying to second-guess it.

This way of proceeding—taking up each question only when an answer is possible, and making your choices from as much peace and goodwill as you are capable of—will not control the outcome (your spouse will not necessarily stay with you, stop the affairs, etc.), but you will be far less likely to complicate

NOTE: If you wish to study the subject of decision making in more depth, see the section and exercise on pages 123–26 of *Notes on How to Live in the World . . . and Still Be Happy.*

the circumstances by acting unnecessarily, and the measures you do take will strengthen and clarify your purpose of love.

Revenge Fantasies

Another state that commonly develops after one learns of an affair is a preoccupation with revenge fantasies and depression. These episodes may entail your spouse, the other participant, or people who seem not to be related at all but whom you suddenly find yourself thinking of angrily or wistfully. Again, do not fight your mind. Your spouse *did* betray you, as did the other party unless that individual had no knowledge or a false picture of your marriage. So do not try to be dishonest with yourself about what occurred. For some, and perhaps for you, a betrayal of this sort can seem as traumatic as a death, and the emotional aftermath can also be as varied and unpredictable. This need not be controlled; merely do not feed and indulge it. If you see that you are extremely sad, are having a revenge fantasy, are excited or apprehensive, or are experiencing any other form of mental defensiveness, merely switch channels. Go to the part of your mind that is a little calmer, a little happier. You may be able to do this only for a few seconds before your reactive emotions blare forth again, but if you will continue to make the effort, not battling, but turning to the light, you will gradually gain ground and at any instant there is always the possibility of being flooded with the complete freedom of forgiveness.

Use any device to make this switch from reaction to being that facilitates the change. Do not waste time looking for the perfect method. If chanting helps, use it. If deep breathing helps, use it. Perhaps you would prefer focusing on some honest and strengthening idea such as "I am not alone," or "Now my peace comforts me," or "My peace connects me to the source of all love, all strength, all certainty," or "Gentleness is my way," or "To see innocence is my release." Do not allow your unhappiness to so confuse you that you come to believe that because someone makes a mistake—and betrayal is always a mistake—he or she is not innocent. Innocence is a permanent condition of the heart toward which all life moves. You cannot judge because you do not know. But you can forgive because forgiveness means to not consider, to not dwell on, to not harbor, to let go, to relinquish, to release. And this you can do without recourse to insincere arguments or to interminable questions of why the individuals behaved in this manner. You wish a free and clean mind as uncluttered with worry and self-reproach as with censure, and this is available to you a few seconds at a time. Take the few seconds and add to them. Simply try. And never be afraid of repeating an effort.

The Affair and Its Effects Are One

At first it may be very difficult for the spouse who is having the affair to join in deep sincerity with his or her partner in working to dissolve the problem. Many will not see it as a problem but as their right. Many will claim no intention of betrayal or even harm. Some will say they acted out of love or even from a desire to grow spiritually.

Anything that causes one's partner deep distress, that jeopardizes relationships and puts lives in turmoil is not spiritually motivated and is not loving. Love is without harm, and although some may disagree with an individual who follows its leadings, it is impossible for an act of love to cause widespread chaos and pain. Again this does not make affairs a sin. The lovelessness is not in the activity but in how it is carried out and how received by those who have no choice but to view it in a given light.

You cannot separate an affair from the way those it touches react. It is a whole, and the whole is what you choose. An affair has inescapable connotations about how you view your marriage. You are saying, "I am willing to risk our relationship for this." And that is a loveless thought. Naturally those who expected more of you are upset, and it is this upset, however long it lasts—and it may last a lifetime—that you called down upon yourself when you decided to have sex or become emotionally involved without sex. You may say that the others overreact, and perhaps this is true, but you chose to include overreaction in your life when you chose the affair. This is not to say that now you must suffer and pay for your sins, but you will have to see the valuelessness of an affair *as a whole* before you will be free of its effects. If the affair goes undetected this will still hold true, because the thought behind it will produce estrangement and all the symptoms thereof even though your spouse, or children if you have any, are not aware of the source.

As to whether you should now confess, your choice is as before. You can act either out of fear and need or out of kindness. Which will cause the least degree of separation, telling or not telling? Perhaps to sit quietly and project both courses into the future will give you insight into what will hurt your friendship least. There is no way to *know,* but you can discover what you *believe.* The peace of your heart is your best guide, and the purpose of fantasizing informing your partner and the course of events that follow, and of *not* informing and afterward, is merely to get a clearer sense of your kindest preference, but naturally this will not foretell events.

Suffering Is a Request for Love

The ego's great idol is excitement, and this is what most affairs promise. Since excitement is a form of anticipation, the beginning of an affair is the most liked and only later does the pain it is causing begin to surface. Even then it may seem as if all the confusion circles outside the new relationship but that within its confines there is peace and unconditional love. One of the most common fantasies during this time is that if somehow the two could just run off to an island they would experience the pure happiness of being with each other untouched by the petty demands and histrionics of others.

As the situation becomes more unbearable or the affair breaks up, the partner involved often begins consciously suffering as greatly as his or her spouse. This can take forms other than remorse for the spouse—distress over the general chaos, sadness over the loss of the other person, guilt, confusion over what changes to make, and so on. Seldom is this suffering seen, or if seen, appreciated, by anyone else. He or she had all the fun and now has no reason to complain.

Here is when you need a true friend, and of course the person with whom you had the affair has manifestly poor credentials, and your spouse is not feeling friendly. Trying to rally support for your side of things will do you little good and could cause you to lose your perspective altogether. The work you must begin is to forgive absolutely your spouse, yourself and anyone else who figures prominently in your mind at this time. You did no more or less than make a mistake, and you wish now to end it. You will continue to push your spouse away if you merely switch from attacking others to attacking yourself. Instead, see the value of gentleness and feel its peace and comfort. If you are patient, it is likely that your partner will join you in this work instead of trying to answer desertion with desertion. If not, you can see innocence nonetheless. Be slow to rise to the bait and quick to comfort. Do not try to justify what you did, even in your own mind, because this will only lead to more judgment. Your aim now is to free yourself of the past and join with this one who stayed with you and truly loves you.

Your Joint Plan for Healing

We have helped many couples past this unhappy dynamic and know that it can be solved by any two who are willing to stop blaming and defending and settle down to work. It is a problem just like any other and requires no special approach. Both partners must begin by assuming their participation in the difficulty, set about studying the dynamic in a nonjudgmental way, and devise a plan to move beyond it.

Although only one partner has the affair, the other reacts, and except for this there would perhaps be little damage. The reaction, of course, is as blameless as the affair and neither could have been avoided given the couple's level of progress. But now more is seen than was before and both are ready to choose again.

It is not necessary to try to define how one spouse "drove" the other to it, what was unfair in the reaction, who should or should not have been told, and so forth. You are not embarked on a search for all possible faults and injustices. Rather you wish to see plainly what the emotions were that led both of you away from friendship and what your deeper feelings and beliefs are that, if they had been attended to, would have prevented these mistakes. Your real emotions must be experienced and not merely named, and to do this a daily practice period is usually necessary.

Once or twice a day, for as many weeks or months as necessary, sit together and look into your hearts for what you really think and feel about the bond between you. Go over and over this ground, for with each effort at seeing, your vision will improve. Ask yourselves, silently or together, what real friendship and commitment are. Do not try to make rigid rules about this, but *see* what devotion is made of, what it feels like, how it guides you, where it takes you. You are attempting to sink deeper into yourself—so deep that you can find a place where mistakes of this sort become impossible so unwilling are you to hurt each other.

It will protect trust and improve your concentration on the work before you if the stimulus of the other man or woman involved has been removed, and perhaps this is something you will discover for yourselves during your preliminary period of examining all aspects of the problem. It is unfair to this other person for even a little relationship to continue. Also, it is expecting too much of your marriage and of the ego of the partner who had the affair for him or her to continue seeing this other person. All communication of any sort should stop. If a complete break with this individual is not feasible, then contact should be lessened as severely as possible and strictly limited to those times when other people are present. This kind of buffer is needed to keep the false emotions from becoming stirred up and mental confusion once again setting in.

You may discover additional aids to healing as you go along. Occasionally, but this is very individual, an open talk between all parties involved can be helpful in clearing the air and furnishing the necessary perspective for beginning the more sustained effort that your daily practice periods will provide. Chapter VII on old patterns can be a very helpful supplement if the problem is chronic. Other gestures that could be included in your plan may occur to you, but any measure you take should be decided together and without coercion.

FINANCES

Treasuring Your Relationship

Whenever a list of the most common marital problems is published, issues over money often head the list. Yet how could this be? Isn't money just strips of paper with funny faces? Like sex, physical appearance, romance and other possessions, money is closely linked in people's minds with happiness. If we could have anything in the world we wanted we would be happy—or so it is believed by most. But since no one ever has or could find himself in that position, the corollary belief is that the more we have the happier we are. The fact that there is not one atom of evidence to support this has not deterred the human race from believing it ardently for thousands of years. Money buys things. More money buys more and better things. You are the reason I have less money. You are the cause of my unhappiness. And indeed this insane logic keeps a very large percentage of long-term relationships in turmoil.

Interestingly, it often is not an issue in the short-term relationship. A couple can do quite well without a running argument over money, yet once they marry they cannot get through a single week without it. As long as their future was in doubt, they had reason to fantasize that marriage and the assurance of a permanent partner would give them happiness. On discovering that marriage cannot *give,* they turn to some other external condition, and money is an ancient and convenient target.

Being such a peculiar and contrived little thing to symbolize so much, money is one of the better examples illustrating that we are never upset for the reason we think. Whenever financial questions come between you, remember that this entire subject is riddled with false issues and base your solutions on something more sustaining than a mere manipulation of numbers. If you decide to try a joint checking account, see that the true purpose is trust and make trust your priority. If the plan is to divide funds and have separate accounts, realize that your deeper aim is to extend appreciation and respect, and make this treasuring of each other the end you seek. If one partner agrees to cut back on certain expenditures or to take on more work for more income, be certain this is a gift to the relationship offered in grace and happiness and not a sacrifice that conceals a hidden price.

Undercutting Money

When I began work toward a Ph.D. I was surprised to discover that (during that era) in most graduate schools, psychology was not a discipline concerned with the problems of people. In the university I attended there had to be an opening in one of the departments of psychology before a student could complete the doctoral program. Two departments openly hostile to each other invited me to join them. One ran rats through mazes, the other studied pigeons in Skinner boxes, and the friends I had made there assured me that to have the option of both these great pursuits was most fortunate. I evidently became so grateful that within days I developed a severe duodenal ulcer and had to drop out.

While I was convalescing it occurred to me that perhaps I could write books without a Ph.D., and so I asked Gayle if she would take a job and support us while I tried to get published. This she did for two years, at the end of which time I had a book out that was selling well enough for us to live on. At that time in the South for Gayle to agree to such a role was a heroic offer, but as more books were written and our income increased, her contribution of a mere two years dwindled in my esteem. Eventually the total earnings I could point to and the years of work I had amassed left no doubt that my debt to her had been paid many times over and that the present distribution of financial rights was patently unfair. Periodically we would argue over who had the final say on large purchases, how our wills must read, should Gayle get a job, or should she be provided with a set income. Even the question of a postmarital financial agreement came up.

Around seven or eight years into our marriage we reached a point where it was obvious that our lives were being made miserable over our preoccupation with money and we had to find a way to drop it. This was the turning point, because it was the first time we had seen that we were united on not wanting to be unhappy. The problem was not with each other but was a clashing of little selves outside our vital need for peace.

We did come up with a plan and it succeeded in removing the issue, but it is not one that would necessarily fit any other couple's personalities and circumstances. Each ego, each set of needs, must be examined and well-tailored means found for the partners to care for each other.

We saw that there were at least two ways to nullify all disagreements over money. One was for Gayle to say, "It is your money and I will do whatever you wish about it." The other was for me to say, "It is our money—all yours and all mine—and I will not question anything you do with it, neither will you question me."

At first these positions seemed too extreme, and yet the condition of our relationship was also extreme, so we each tried to see if either was something we could live with. I realized immediately that although it seemed to be approximately what I had been asking of Gayle, I did not want her in a subservient role even if she was willing to assume one. Furthermore, I saw that if we were to consider everything Gayle's, there would undoubtedly be times when she would spend money in ways that I would not, but I honestly did not believe she would bankrupt us. I was surprised to find myself admitting that Gayle was actually more responsible fiscally than I was. Being the sole contributor to our income did not make me wiser than the noncontributor! I therefore proposed the second alternative and we joined checkbooks and bank accounts, threw in cash gifts from relatives at birthdays, and even agreed that any inheritances we received individually would be ours together.

For about the first year I had difficulty accepting my own proposal, but every time I wavered, the thought of returning to our former state of dissension put me back on course and now, twelve years later, I do not understand what my fear was about.

By no means are we recommending this particular solution to anyone. We give it merely as an example that these kinds of problems can be resolved if both parties are determined to see that their happiness together is more important than money and then set about devising ways to meet each other's ego needs without threatening the relationship's financial stability.

Row Gently

You do not want to go through life struggling with your relationship, struggling with your health, struggling with your children, struggling with your finances. An easy and peaceful way to proceed becomes obvious when two join their strengths. Do not make the mistake that many new-age couples are now making of joining weaknesses. Do not tell each other that everything is going to work out, that all you have to do is "trust." Save yourself the lesson of having to learn that you do not somehow possess special knowledge or a charmed life. Row your financial boat gently down the stream. Nothing is proved by struggling against the ways and means of the world such as earning, saving and budgeting. Be prudent as well as generous, because the two are not in conflict.

There are probably couples who go through life oblivious of where their money goes and where it will come from and who are also consistently centered and peaceful, but like the couples who decide they can flaunt the ordinary sexual customs, it usually does not end well. Perhaps the biggest cause of financial difficulty is arrogance. "Somehow I know better than others"—and yet what a petty field of honor money is. It has been Gayle's and my experience that the Eastern philosophy of "Make your living with your left foot" is encouraging of simple happiness and peace. In other words, money isn't the focus of life; therefore, *do* whatever is required not to think about it.

HAVING CHILDREN

Children Are Wonderful and Much More

Children are indeed wonderful. At times they seem to be connected to a source beyond the reach of mere adults, and so when John came into the living room the other day and said, "Would you like to know the ancient secret of beans?" Gayle and I listened very carefully.

"If you open both ends of the can, they push right out," he said, and went back to his rock collection (which is slowly filling the house).

Last night at dinner Jordan, who has only been talking for a
year, gave the blessing. "Be happy and have ketchup," he said,
with his eyes squinted shut in deep earnestness. Jordan is the
member of the family who wants all of us together all the time.
He makes sure that John does not sleep a minute later than
anyone else. If asked whether he wishes to stay home or ride
with the person going into town, he becomes very emotional
and wants to know why we can't all go. And if an argument
breaks out in the house, he starts saying, "I'm sorry! I'm
sorry!" to end it, even though he is not involved.

Children are little lights and constantly remind us all of a
simpler way. Gayle and I cannot fathom how we went for
twelve years without wanting any. We were one of those couples who didn't think they should be allowed in restaurants
and who abruptly changed seats if we noticed one near us in a
movie. It was probably only luck, for we certainly did not
understand the principle, that we first considered having a
child after our marriage had become stable and happy. The
usual tendency is to grasp at children as a way of bridging a
widening gap or merely as a means of perking up a relationship that has grown a little stale.

These are tragic and eminently unsuccessful reasons for
having a baby. But to people who don't know or who have
forgotten, babies are dolls that never need batteries. They lie in
pastel cribs and coo and, when you pass by, look up and smile
at you. You can gather them into your arms and rock them
and then feed them strained plums with a teeny spoon. Friends
and relatives come to your house and congratulate you in low
voices, and leave little presents behind.

All this is in fact true, but overlooked is the nausea, expense
and pain of the pregnancy and birth, the unimaginable exhaustion afterward that for some can last for over a year, the endless diaper changes, the months of interrupted sleep, the unex-
plainable and interminable crying, colic, ear infections,
constipation, rashes, teething, reactions to inoculations, and
on and on, all blanketed in an oppressive anxiety over what to

do now for this very fragile little life around which so many conflicting opinions swirl.

And do not believe that these troubles are magically wiped away by a Leboyer birth, breast-feeding, all-cotton diapers and freezing your own baby food, all of which we and most of our friends tried. The simple fact is that babies are so surprisingly demanding, expensive, tiring and time consuming that they will make any bad relationship worse. Neither can you merely wait it out until they are two. For most of "today's moderns," the twos are terrible and it's all downhill from there—until you come to adolescence, which is the pits.

If you are a couple who enjoy being spontaneous, who like a clean house and a good night's sleep, who want your dinners and TV programs without interruptions, and who are just barely making it with the expenses you already have, then you should consider carefully the effects of a complete alteration of your life-style for the next eighteen years. Most of the changes will not be in the direction of what our society is now picturing as a happy and fulfilling life.

A Baby Will Not Perk Up Your Relationship

But didn't we just say that children are wonderful? Most assuredly—if they are an extension of your love and oneness, in which case they are still every bit as burdensome but now you are in a mental position to see their other side, which is a light and joy so bright that you will find yourself crying at times in profound thanks that these little teachers have come to live with you.

Not only will a baby not add spice to your life or recapture that oneness you both once felt, it is unfair to try to use a baby in this way. The thought of having a child should arise from satisfaction and not from stirrings of discontent, and yet seldom is this the pattern. It is believed (and this is inadvertently fed by the vignettes one reads and hears such as those at the beginning of this chapter) that somehow a child will cover the distance between the partners. If a child is thought of as a bridge, it will be walked on, and this you do not want. It cannot but fail as a substitute for love and it *will* be blamed, probably for the rest of its life. I speak as one who has felt this disappointment, and I am in the majority. It is difficult to reverse these expectations once the child is born. So if possible, gain your clarity before, and do not let your excitement over the prospect of change rob you of the hours of patient and careful examination of your motives that are needed to assure your baby a place and not a position in your home.

If you already have children, it will strengthen your bond with your partner if you will watch your mind for these very common but often unconscious thoughts: "This is not the child I deserve." "I would do better with another kind of child." "This child is lacking." These thoughts lead automatically to "This child should suffer," and love has very little chance of growing amid judgment directed at what you and your partner have made. There is a just-rightness, a flawlessly tailored blessing in the children we receive, but recognition of this is sometimes long in coming. Save yourselves that time by giving what you probably did not receive as a child: unqualified appreciation. If you will nourish this little extension of your and your partner's love, your child will blossom, and rather than being a bridge between you it will be a garland of amusements and joys binding you together.

Common Dynamics

Many are the ways that couples use children to make themselves unhappy. The essence of these problems, as with all others, is that a new range of excuses is found for the couple to turn against each other. Very often, because of the baby's need to be with its mother, to be held by her, breast-fed and so forth, a pattern develops of the woman being left with all the responsibilities and chores that child care entails. Many women unconsciously participate in perpetuating this arrangement through feelings of guilt that no matter how much they do, they still have not reached the hazy ideal of what a mother should be. Men often have inherited the matching expectation, and so the dynamic forms—the woman no longer has time to do any of the things that make her happy, she and her husband are apart much of the time, she is tired, her appearance may not be what she would like, and the baby, not yet much of a companion, cannot make up for it.

For the woman to "fight for her rights" is not the answer that leads to love, but she must be willing to be open and free of embarrassment about indicating those areas in which she needs relief. It falls to the husband not to allow this pattern to develop in the first place, by helping with the child in every conceivable way. Both must sit down together often and discuss the difficulties that have arisen and not let the situation slide, under the assumption that when the child is a little older, all will resolve naturally.

If it is at all possible, time should be regularly scheduled for the two of you to be alone together in ways that are relaxing and pleasurable so that the separation of bodies that an infant often causes does not take on an unhealthy symbolism that in the years to come is never quite shaken.

Another pattern that you should be alert to is the woman, because she is the mother, coming to believe that she knows better than her husband about all things concerning child care. There is no one way to do anything, and both partners must learn to trust and to let the other do it his or her own way during that person's time to be with the child. Unless you believe that it will truly damage the child in some long-term way, remember that love between its mother and father is more important to it than whether its chin is clean, it sleeps on its stomach or back, or is tossed in the air three days before Dr. Spock recommends. If something is extremely anxiety provoking, then mention it, but in a gentle way, remembering that the reason for removing anxiety is to make room for more goodwill between you.

The reverse of this dynamic is for the husband to come home after work and make pronouncements. He hears the baby crying in the other room and points out to his wife, collapsed on the living room couch smoking a cigarette, that crying too long can damage its little psyche and that nicotine enters breast milk. If he really feels that something must be discussed, he should bring it up at a more felicitous moment and in true humility.

The world is in a paroxysm of anxiety over how children should be reared, what they should eat, how they should be dressed, schooled, companioned, played with, disciplined. No one can agree, and all deliver their opinions like blows of a gavel even though they will reverse themselves in forty days. The one thing you do know is that an environment of consideration is more salutary to your child than dissension.

As the child grows older, new dynamics arise from the old. The mother and child may begin forming a special bond that excludes the father. Possibly for very good reasons, the woman turns to the child for her meaning in life. She clings to it and lives for it, and she and the child are a unit that looks down on the father. He comes to feel like an interloper in his own house who can do nothing right. This is as unhappy a pattern as husband and wife forming an alliance against the child, which is especially common toward an adolescent. All the couple's troubles are traced to "the little monster." Were it not for it, the bills would be met, the garbage taken out on schedule, and they could be creative and "interested in life" for a change.

Again, each of these dynamics is a form of separation. Yet nothing justifies turning against a member of the family. All decisions concerning the child must come from unity or else the mind of the child as well as the minds of the couple are segregated. To argue before your child, reverse decisions that your partner has made, take sides with the child against some injustice by the other will teach only the lessons we have all been learning for generations. Let the insanity end with *this* child in *this* family. If you need to write out a contract between you that, for example, you will make no unilateral decisions concerning your children, then do so and abide by it with the appreciation for harmony and clarity that inspired it.

Another Spouse's Children

The problem of a former spouse's child within the relationship can be handled in the same united way, even though this circumstance tends to be a little more difficult because of additional and quite unrealistic expectations. The partner who is not the biological parent is often looked to for feelings that in most cases are simply not possible. A bond does not exist and should not be expected to form quickly or at all. However, it is always possible for that person to be a true friend to the child, to treat it gently, and to understand that it too cannot magically generate emotional ties it does not feel. Stripped of romantic nonsense, these relationships have a potential for mutual caring and understanding, and there is always the possibility that in time a bond can form that equals in depth and loveliness the one that is sometimes found between parent and child.

Often we have little difficulty accepting as a given the nature of the relationship between our spouse and his or her parents and siblings. It existed prior to the marriage, we recognize it, and do not feel the need to pass judgment. With the child of our spouse, because it is still influenceable, the temptation is to think we must make our imprint, we must enter the child's mind and take our rightful place. This is not necessary, and the more peaceful and therefore more loving approach is for the stepparent to assume a primarily supportive role and to try to appreciate rather than criticize the existing relationship between parent and child.

The child will naturally be anxious about all the changes that are occurring and especially about this new person with authority over his or her life. For the child already frightened by change, even though the fear may be well camouflaged, the fewer alterations made in routine, the easier the transition will be, and this applies especially to the child's ways of being with the natural parent. If some aspect of this relationship is truly destructive, there will be time for gentle consideration of this after the child is more settled and feels that he or she does indeed have a niche in life and a place in the hearts of both parents.

The biological parent of course does not want to form an alliance against the new spouse. Therefore this person should watch carefully for thoughts that somehow he or she is being called upon to choose between the two. The belief that someone must lose can be very strong in these situations. Any demand the world makes on you to take sides can be safely neglected. A family of parents and children functions best when parents fulfill their role as the decision makers and, as with two natural parents, there is less room for ego activity if they always do this as one. This is not taking sides against the child because, at least until adolescence, children feel cared for if they are provided gentle, firm direction and not cared for if given the latitude to do anything at all that occurs to them. It is simply a characteristic of the child mind that consistency, if it is not rigid or overwhelming, is a strong symbol of love and safety.

In dealing with these or the many other possibilities of problems concerning children, the principle is to unite in love in order to avoid the new opportunities to separate and to hand-in-hand gaze directly at the difficulty until no areas of unawareness remain. Then open your minds to any simple solution and begin your walk past the problem.

As always, the key is to support each other, to be each other's complete friend. Thus you assure that your child will be left with an image of you that will guide her or him safe and sure for a lifetime, and not with one that must be surmounted before a real family can be established.

"I NEED MY OWN SPACE"

Mental Separateness

Because of the emphasis we have been giving friendship over separateness, it would be easy to conclude that Gayle and I are advocating that a couple never leave each other's side. But, as we have also tried to make clear, we are speaking of mental, not physical, closeness. Whether bodies are together is unimportant—except as it influences feelings of connectedness within each partner. Thus to not sleep together would be unthinkable to some, whereas to others, because for example one person is a light sleeper, doing so would consistently put that partner in a bad mood.

There are no rules as to whether a couple should run errands together, go to parties together, vacation together or even live in the same home. For a number of years Gayle and I had separate, adjoining houses which we built ourselves for precisely this purpose. We each had our own bedroom, kitchen and bathroom and there was only one door between, which either of us could close. In those days we were both temperamental writers whose creative flow could be plugged by even the brush of pant legs within a few meters of our yellow pads. Now there are four of us and we not only live in the same house but all sleep in the same room and, depending on the number of monsters hanging out, on the same spot in the same bed.

At this time there are two conflicting values about togetherness. The old notion that the more a couple is around each other and touch each other, the greater is their love, is still a thought strongly present in most people's minds. Opposed to it is the new-age value of "doing your own thing," "having your own space," "owning your own power." This second standard is linked with self-actualization, creativity, spiritual growth

and a meaningful life. To oversimplify, the two values are romance and power. And both are purely an appearance. Naturally there is more substance than this to these concepts, but
the destructive side of them is essentially "we should do everything together" versus "we should do everything apart." And
both positions cause estrangement.

Possibly it is easier to see how those partners who at every
juncture insist on being physically apart precipitate estrangement than those who are always pushing for nearness. Yet
both pit wills against one another. "I want you by my side
even if you don't want to be because I love you so much" is a
position as crazy as it is commonplace. Many who do not
think they are participating in the causes of a divorce are in
fact pushing their spouse further away by a constant stream of
demands to "talk with me," "see me more," "move back into
the house," "stop associating with so-and-so"—all of which is
an attempt to bring about a picture of unity at the expense of
its content. It is more difficult to love someone who insists that
you must do what you don't want to do, and this is the deterrent that forcing bodies together sets in place.

Using a Symbol's Power

Earlier we said that the meaning physical closeness has lies in
its effect on each partner's sense of oneness. It is a sign that has
personal significance only. But it must not be ignored or its
effects will operate unseen. In most relationships the power of
symbols is overlooked because many of them are now widely
recognized as symbols. For example, a marriage ceremony is a
symbol, and most people do not understand why they have
such difficulty after a divorce if what was terminated was a
contract, a hollow sanction of the state, a mere piece of paper.
But for thousands of years it has been deeply believed that a
marriage is made in heaven, that it is the very will of God, and
on an unconscious level most of those who profess to place no

meaning in the state of matrimony believe they are violating a sacred trust if they abandon their spouse, for whatever cause.

This is one reason a relationship that appears to be responsible for the breakup of a marriage is more difficult to sustain than one formed by two who were uncommitted to others at the time they came together. The ego has a foothold, and although the two may profess not to feel guilty, the belief in guilt is more deeply rooted than they may realize and an enormous effort will be needed to forgive and bless themselves as well as those who may appear to have been hurt.

It is not the function of this book to argue theology, and so we intentionally are not offering an opinion on whether a marriage is "really" divinely sanctioned, but we do wish to point out that many, and perhaps on some level all, can be long disturbed if they disregard their feelings about this symbol and think they can reason away the impact of history.

A parallel example is the trial separation. Often overlooked is the profound picture of desertion that is presented to the mind when one partner moves out. This causes deep feelings of estrangement that are not expected, and very few marriages survive this seemingly needed and reasonable "little breather."

Marriage is an extreme example of the unconscious effect of symbols, and certainly no couple should stop themselves from seeking a divorce out of fear, but if the power of a mental picture can be recognized here, then perhaps the effect of lesser symbols can be respected and, more important, used as aids in maintaining the mental strength and happiness that are potential in any relationship.

Another effect can be seen when one spouse leaves the house for a few hours. Note the degree of closeness you feel before, and then note carefully what you feel for the first few minutes after coming together. The effects of symbols are very individual, but generally speaking, it is never true that "absence makes the heart grow fonder." Absence may sometimes spur the ego to greater *longing* but its usual effect on the "heart" is to cause a slight but discernible distance. Obviously the answer is not to refuse any job that cannot be done at home, to never go on a preschool field trip without your husband, or to insist that your wife become a member of the touch football team. But if you will take a moment to greet each other when one of you returns home, perhaps sit down and visit as you would with a friend or acquaintance you had invited in,—just a few seconds to indicate that seeing the other is more important than asking anxious questions or voicing worries over petty concerns—then the ego is short-circuited and the influence of what is meaningless truly becomes meaningless in the light of obvious love.

We are not proposing some ritual or even meaning to single out a couple's daily comings and goings for special attention. The overall effect of being apart physically should simply be observed rather than ignored merely because it "shouldn't" matter. Thus at a social event or at someone's house whom one or both of you finds difficult, perhaps you will notice that if you sit or stand near your spouse, or just "check in" every now and then, it is easier for you to get through the occasion and you feel less withdrawn from each other afterward. It is now considered sophisticated to divide couples at dinner tables, and if a point is made of this, Gayle and I do not fight it, but if someone's seating arrangement will not be spoiled, we always opt for corniness—while also not being so outwardly affectionate that others feel excluded and strange. Another couple might prefer taking advantage of the opportunity to talk to friends they haven't seen for a while and so would be more peaceful sitting apart. The only rule is peace. The more peaceful your choices, the more your love grows. Even though most relationships are placed under a slight stress from even short absences, they can also be agitated from too much contact and so specific guidelines must always be tentative.

Ways of Joining

With this in mind we would like to give you a few more ways of expressing the desire to join that we and some of the couples we have worked with have found practical. We first noticed the general effectiveness of a "joining break" with John and Jordan. Young children have not yet learned socially acceptable ways of showing unhappiness and often act it out in what appears to be defiant behavior. We discovered early on that to pat or hug or in some other gentle way show one of our boys that we loved them would sometimes stop the behavior as if by magic and discipline was made unnecessary. It also tends to hold true that opposition to what one's mate is saying or doing is often inappropriate. To see beyond the irritation, the complaining or whatever other behavior we interpret as negative, to the fact that our partner is feeling cut off, and then to offer consideration instead of advice, can frequently produce a similar magic. It should not matter that, for example, when a wife starts rubbing her husband's back, he "knows what she is up to"—for love is never truly calculating in an ego sense. Of course if the gesture is made merely to get the other to shut up then it is not motivated by love.

These little moments of joining, expressed in whatever ways are pleasant and unpretentious, can come after an argument, during an illness, following a difficult phone conversation, or in response to any other circumstance that tends to make one feel alone. They are pointless, of course, if one partner objects, pressure and peace being incompatible.

Another enjoyable way we have of joining is a once-a-week date. We hire a baby-sitter, leave early and often get home past our usual bedtime. During the week we try to eat an excellent diet, one we have worked out for ourselves over the past several years, but on these evenings we allow whatever we want with the one exception of alcohol. Our "date" consists merely of a few simple activities we both like, such as going to dinner, taking a walk, buying ice cream cones. It is strictly for the two of us because our purpose is to practice thoroughly enjoying each other's company, and the difference this one conscientiously observed symbol has made in our relationship is astounding.

Three other practices that we alluded to earlier are a short period on awakening during which we decide our spiritual purpose for the day and meditate on it, a long meditation in the afternoon, and a brief time just before falling asleep in which we sit up and release anything that we may still be carrying from the day. The latter we do silently, and often John joins us, while Jordan smiles indulgently.

Often we will pause before leaving and after returning in the car or before and after going into a store or other building. We call this "bracketing," and the purpose is merely to maintain a simple, focused, easy state of mind.

An occasion for joining that we have found essential to a sustained peace between us is just after having been with an individual or couple who have relationship problems. Our observation is that as two people's egos weaken, their sensitivity to the unhappiness of those they come in contact with, even on the phone or in meditation, increases, and although this allows them to be more effective counselors and teachers, to some extent they become like sponges that soak up everyone else's problems.

If you are alert to it, this will be especially apparent after social occasions or after a visit with an old friend whose relationship is foundering or has broken up. This certainly does not mean that you withhold your help and love, or refuse to counsel, but that you are careful not to join on the level of conflict and pain and bring this back with you.

You might consider joining together very soon after the contact, to formally release what one or both of you has taken on. Otherwise you are likely to begin mimicking the identical state of mind with no awareness of its source.

Helping Make It Easier

The world is not an easy place to live in and this becomes increasingly apparent as we go along. Eventually we see that it is impossible to live happily without help. Help comes in many forms but surely one of the most easily recognizable is a long-term relationship. Yet so often it only seems to make matters worse. This pattern is not natural and you wish now to be done with it. You want to find ways to make life easier for your friend. You want to become a partnership, a team that pulls together to get through life.

To do this you must acknowledge each other's strengths and allow the relationship to use them the way a mind uses all parts of a body. There is no competition between limbs because each is in a position to do some things more easily. Likewise, one partner is good at turning down invitations and so that one gladly takes on the task without thinking less of the partner who finds it more difficult. The other partner can remove insects with less anxiety and so is happy to do this for the relationship. In large and small ways you help, and possibly the largest is in meeting each other's needs. "I need my own space" is a need and it must be met. Obviously you do not wish to feed and expand it, but to ignore it is asking for trouble. I need to shop, I need to meditate, I need to masturbate, I need one night a week with the girls, I need tennis with the boys,—all may be of the ego to the degree that they spring from feelings of incompleteness. But unless they can be peacefully discarded they had better be met or else the ego begins to grow, which means the differences between you grow.

Obviously some needs could be quite injurious to your particular relationship and cannot be met in the old ways. But never is there one way only of meeting a need. I need to get drunk; I need to be promiscuous; I need to be right at all costs; I need to shoplift; I need to hit; I need to control every situation—can all be redirected into harmless channels.

Look at the need together. Inspect it. Reduce it to bare bones. Get help in this if necessary. A need to shoplift may more basically be a need for danger. Danger may be a need for excitement. There are many ways to have a vivid sense of danger and excitement without threatening the stability of one's family and the peace of mind of one's partner. Usually the need will not be this dramatic, but the consequences of one partner condemning rather than helping to meet even a very small need can be equally disastrous.

Gayle needs to be freed of all responsibilities the day before her period. For years we ignored this and as a result, many severe and needless fights occurred on those days. Now we have a sacred rule that on the day Gayle announces that it's coming, I take over all housework and child care, Gayle gets into the car (she loves to drive), buys a bag of Famous Amos cookies and a Pepsi Free (the idols of all her taste buds), and goes to town to harvest the malls. I have eliminated my need for naps through exercise and improved diet, but I still want to get to bed early and read for half an hour or so. If I see I am going to miss this I have a hard time not becoming preoccupied and irritable. Thus it is that at 8 P.M. water, toothpaste and discarded clothes fill the air and a scampering of many large and small feet can be heard heading for the bedroom. Jordan has a need to be held in a special way after waking. John has a need for "rough time" after dinner. We have finally learned not to question these and many other peculiarities of each of our separate egos, but rather to use these differences as ways of joining, so that small insanities become sanities within a loving relationship.

In a sense all needs are the ego's desire to withdraw from love, which is killing it. Even Jordan's yearning to be held, if it were to grow and become inflexible, which unmet needs tend to do, could hinder the formation of real relationships. This is why each partner must guard against turning a need into a right. I have no right to be angry if on some evenings circumstances do not allow for an early bedtime. I have no right to cite my need and use it as a club to get my way. If it is gradually being forgotten by the rest of the family and I can feel my ego feeding on this neglect, then I must bring it up, for to pretend I am now beyond it when obviously I am not could precipitate a major flare-up that would be much more disturbing to the family than their being conscientious in helping me.

The aim in meeting needs is peace, and if at times they cannot be met, then peace and not defense of the needs must be our choice. Ego desires cannot be justified because they hold no love. If they are trimmed down as much as possible to start with, met in nonthreatening ways, and acknowledged and treated as opportunities to be caring by the partner who is stronger in those areas, they will lessen and eventually fade completely. If they are resisted by the one who has them, if they are overindulged, or if they are judged by one's partner, they are made more prominent and real in the mind. Because the instinct is to defend whatever is attacked, looking down on another's need tends to strengthen that person's identification with it. And naturally self-attack has the same consequence. So do not be embarrassed to discuss these subjects openly. It is a gift of trust as well as a protection to do so. Learn the sweet warm feeling that comes of understanding and being understood. Meeting each other's needs does not have to be a confusing concept.

GROWING OLD TOGETHER

Your Partner Is a Mirror

As we have become more youth conscious, the divorce rate has risen. It is no longer uncommon for unions that have lasted half a century to break up suddenly. There are many reasons for this, but the increasing disgust with old age is fundamental. In fairy tales the wicked witch was invariably old, but now even the power of wisdom, the respect for experience, is denied the elderly. If we had witches today it would be the young graduate witches versed in the latest advances in magic who would be respected. Old age no longer has a single redeeming value in our society. It and all that goes with it is viewed as a curse.

Who would want to be reminded that every day he slips deeper into an anathema? And yet, unless there is a growing love to see, that is what each partner reminds the other of. Not verbally, of course. And not in the little pretenses of youth retained—the aimless activeness, the drinking habits, a new hair color, perhaps even a youthful, blind embracing of all the latest concepts and beliefs—but in the reflection of inexorable physical change. The desperate clutching to symptoms of youth makes the mirror that each holds up to the other's aging all the more unforgiving, because the failure to stay young is plainly seen by one's long-time intimate who cannot be fooled. He or she knows that the other's hair is thinning, the breasts are sagging, the stomach dropping, the memory slipping, the sexual organs becoming unarousable, the digestion demanding an ever higher price for indulgences.

Seen also are the defeats of a lifetime: business failures, failure to achieve the social status wanted, unrealized hopes for the children. So often the elderly wear defeat. They put it on in the morning. And especially the aging partner looks defeated in the other's eyes because that person's boasts, heard so frequently in earlier years, are now a mockery and every abandoned effort is silently recollected. Bodies fail—this is the law of bodies. And because to our ego a relationship is a union of bodies, we believe relationships also must fail.

Little wonder that the heart slowly turns to stone. Appreciation dies. The affections shrink and harden. Now all you get from your spouse is an occasional dry kiss on the cheek and a few little courtesies. Before, when your body was young, everything you wore was wonderful. You could do nothing wrong with your hair. Where did the appreciation go, the little compliments that made one feel confident and good? Now before going out for the evening you must ask how you look, and the response never quite reassures.

Becoming As a Child

Most older couples do not realize how influenced they have been by the values of our time and how absolutely they turn against each other. Instead of being a friend and helping one another age happily, they shut off the gestures that are most needed. Perhaps this is why the elderly frequently turn to children with such ardor. A young child will not recoil. They are not afraid to touch old people, to kiss them on the mouth, to say they like their hat, or to ask if their swollen fingers hurt and to discuss it all with them.

Very often small children recognize the priceless gifts that older people have to offer: time and full attention. Most younger adults never give their children absolute time. They talk or play while partly engaged in some other task or they good-naturedly endure the wasted minutes until they can get to things of greater interest or concern. As they age, many people become increasingly aware that one thing the world has plenty of is time. Before, it seemed to be always running out. But this was an illusion created by running people.

If the older couple could take what they have learned and give it to each other, these truly could be "golden years." But each waits for the other to make the first gesture or shuts down if the initial efforts are not honored with sufficient thanks and reciprocity. There *is* an alternative: to start in little ways, quiet and gentle ways, and to yield not to depression and discouragement. Just a little touching, with great sensitivity to what is wanted; a few appreciations shown more warmly, more genuinely; an offer perhaps to take over a task not traditionally your own and then carried out easily and with the pleasure that comes of helping. Naturally these attempts will feel strained and insincere at first. But kindness is more important than a moment's awkwardness.

The Body's Function

The body is just another way of giving. That is its function—to present the contents of the heart in specific ways that are meaningful to another body. You can do this as effectively through an old body as through a young one. What better time to begin using it in this way now that the limits of its capacity to make you happy are being so honestly seen. Like a telephone, you can utilize the body to give and to receive, but it cannot of itself produce anything of substance, even when it is "full of promise." The time has come to stop thinking of this one limited means as a capacious end. If you long for your dying youth you are of no use to your partner or to yourself.

If the body is a means of communication, what is it saying to your spouse? Have you let yourself go and in effect are you saying, "I don't care what you think"? Isn't it interesting how people will get in shape after a divorce, but while they actually have someone they can't be bothered? Have you stopped caring for your health? If so, your body may communicate mostly misery and complaints. Is your smoking or salt intake going to ravage your partner of his or her constant companion years before it was necessary? Are you clinging to the appearance of a younger person's diet? Whom does this fool? Certainly not your body. Why not eat to feel good, to be a little stronger, to have a little more energy—not the fatuous superhealth so faddish today, but enough to be unpreoccupied, enough that you are in a position to lift your partner's spirits rather than dampen them. For whom do you dress? For whom do you drive? Are you using your body to increase fear or lessen it? You know how hard it is to be old. So bend to help one person, not to hold up the world.

And how do you look upon the body of your partner? The idea that age is wicked and ugly does not have to be believed, no matter how many billboards, bumper stickers, paperbacks, TV ads, magazines and songs imply otherwise. The notion that an old human is repulsive is wholly groundless, and many artists, especially the masters of earlier eras, clearly did not see age the way we have come to think is obligatory. And we are quite arbitrary in applying this perception to humans. Old trees and buildings are often revered for their age, and the lines of time and experience etched in any elderly person's face can be seen for exactly what they are rather than as symbols of lost sexiness, athleticism and promotability.

In many ways the body itself becomes wiser as the mind that occupies it matures. It is more intelligently sensitive to foods and fears, activities and stresses and sends out stronger, less equivocal signals of even little dangers to its health and mental balance. The wisdom is there to be seen and it is not mental dodgery to behold it in your partner. "How does my partner look compared to others?" can give way to gentle appreciation for what these hands, this face has been through. You can *love* your partner's wrinkles if you will look at them. The body before you tells you that this person has tried very hard. It is a map of what he or she has been through, and the efforts of a lifetime deserve deep respect, not silly comparisons. Cherish your partner as a priceless possession. Bless every white hair, every degree of stoop, every line, every blemish and bruise. This person truly loves you, and the vessel that contains love is sacred.

Opportunity of a Lifetime

Humans tell themselves little stories about how life is and especially about how it could be. These of course appear in novels, movie and TV dramas, and song lyrics, and are implied in articles and nonfiction books. In a story an author can control events and make an unworkable ideal seem to work. Being separate is the ideal of our time, and in most modern tales life is meaningful and interesting for the protagonists even though they have never committed themselves wholly to anyone. In fact, most of them have never committed themselves to anything, not even their work, and this is made out to be the basis of their secret for a meaningful life—at least meaningful enough to read page after page or watch week after week. These stories do often include romance, usually unenduring and based always on external specialness: physical appearance, youth, sex, money, being right, and so on. Occasionally "good" long-term relationships are pictured in which the couple has managed to sustain the honeymoon period indefinitely. Somehow they never grow old and feeble, never go through disturbing personality changes, never have severe sexual problems, never lose what makes them separate and superior beings, and this rather than a deep inward bond is the manifest reason they stay together.

The elderly couple have lived a real life. They have tried out many ideals and know that the unworkable does not work. Consequently they have great potential for perspective. Do not lose this opportunity. You see that love is the only sane idea in the world, and you know what love is not.

Now is the occasion for friendship. Look softly at one another, see the burden, and lightly brush it from your companion's shoulders. There are places only you know how to reach. Be each other's healer and saint. Your hands can still touch, your words can bring comfort, your eyes can smile away the fears. If now you do indeed see the world plainly then turn and give where your gifts will be stored, where not one will be lost. Each will kindle a light the other has known before, and side by side you will bask in the warmth of your giving.

Epilogue

The Last Instruction

There was a student who went before his God and said, "You have told me that my training is now complete. You have said that I am ready to enter the world and put theory into form, to move mountains with love. But you who *are* love have given me no instruction in the ways between a man and a woman."

"Yes, my child," said God, "there is a question that saddens you. But do you see it clearly?"

And as he had been trained, the student went within his silence and gathered it about him. And shortly he said, "I have many questions that sadden me. Am I to marry or be alone? And if I am alone, am I to be celebate? And if I am to marry, are we to be alone or with children? And if I have a spouse and children, do they join me in the work you have given me? And if they are to join me, what am I to do if they refuse?"

* * *

"Yes, my child," said God, "these and a thousand questions more could you ask. Yet do you not see a single question beneath all the others?"

Again the student touched his silence, and this time he remained still for a long while. Presently he said, "I believe that the one question I have is 'Am I alone?' "

And God said, "You have seen well. You have seen the only question there is. The world you are about to enter is merely this question."

Still the student did not depart. And God said, "Perhaps, my child, you think you do not know the answer."

The student said, "Are there no thoughts you can give me to answer the little questions that are born of this one?"

"There are indeed," said God, "but they are thoughts to become and not thoughts to think."

And then God smiled and took the student into his arms. And he said, "You are the work you must perform. And whenever you fail in your function you will be alone, and by choice you will abstain from all life, all truth, all reality.

"You will know when you have remembered your function by the love that overwhelms judgment and desire. For love *is* your function: To be love, and see it in others. To give love, and receive it easily. Nothing you say or do in the world will have any meaning without love.

"To love is to be in the shining heart of God and thus within the hearts of the least and the greatest of God's children. For when you are in the heart of God you do not look through the faults of your brother. You do not look past them, or over them, or around them. You look within. For only in your own heart will you recognize the Pulse that courses through every child who has ever come into the world and see that all living things are innocent.

"In the world you will be tempted to believe that to love one you must first love all. But I tell you now that you must love one before you can love all. For there is only one. Take then a spouse, or no spouse. Have children, or none. For your brother is every child, woman, and man you look upon. But until you treat at least one other brother as you would be treated and come to recognize that his heart is your own, you will wander alone through space and time and dream of death. Then will you think of hurting your brother and dream of hurting me. But when at last you wake to who your brother is, you will wake to me.

"During that instant you will return home. And I will sing you the ancient song that dissolves all tears. For you are my child and there is no other. And I will rock you awake to life in me: you who are my joy and my meaning, and without whom I cannot be complete.

"I hold a place in eternity for you where we will dwell, I in you and you in me forever. Until that time, my child, know love, even in the world, and you will know that you are not alone."